Basic Equitation

BASIC EQUITATION

COMMANDANT JEAN LICART

Illustrated by Jean Moreau de Tours

J. A. ALLEN & CO., LTD.
1 LOWER GROSVENOR PLACE
London S.W.1.

British Library Cataloguing in Publication Data

Licart, Jean
Basic equitation.
1. Horsemanship
I. Title
798.2'3   SF309

ISBN 0–85131–202–0

First published in the French language as
Comment Apprendre A Monter A Cheval

English translation copyright © 1966 by
J. A. Allen & Company Limited

First published in this edition 1973
Reprinted 1979
Reprinted 1985

© J. A. Allen & Company Limited, 1966

No part of this book may be reproduced or transmitted in any way or by any means, electronic or mechanical, including photocopy, recording, or any information storage and retrieval system known or to be invented, without permission in writing from the publisher. All rights reserved.

Printed in Great Britain by
Page Bros (Norwich) Limited, Norwich, Norfolk

CONTENTS

GENERAL REFLECTIONS ON RIDING AND HORSES
  I Riding   ix
  II The horse   xii

INTRODUCTION   xv

CHAPTER
  I THE BEGINNER'S REFLEXES   1

  II FIRST LESSON   6
  1. *What you should know before mounting: Safety warnings; saddling, bridling, leading the horse.*
  2. *To horse! Mounting and dismounting. The rider's adjustment: enveloping with the legs. The horse's line of equilibrium. The balance of the upper body. How to use your legs and hands. Feeling the rhythm of the horse's neck movements and the horse's mouth. The halt. Principal suppling exercises.*

  III SECOND LESSON   42
Suppling exercises. Contact with the horse's mouth. Halts. The trot in supple suspension and the posting trot. The sitting trot, raising the toes.

  IV THIRD LESSON   58
Vaulting to mount. Improving the rider's adherence at the trot in supple suspension and at the posting trot. Developing steady hands at the posting trot. Use of the reins. Improving the erectness of the trunk at the sitting trot. Regulating and directing the horse's movements. The opening rein and the indirect rein. Vaulting to dismount.

  V FOURTH LESSON   74
Perfecting the posting trot and adherence at the sitting trot without stirrups. Finding the balance of the upper body, and suppling exercises at the sitting trot

while checking the erectness of the trunk. The control of the horse: moving in different directions; an erect upper body is as necessary to the horse as it is for the rider. The extension of the horse's neck promotes obedience. Principles governing resistance. Action of the rein of opposition. Mechanics of the opening rein.

VI FIFTH LESSON   84

Developing the play of the loins at the sitting trot. Control: Causes of the principal difficulties encountered by beginners. "The haunches alone govern direction." Using the upper body as an aid. Coordinating the action of the body with the outside lateral aids. Strike-offs into the canter.

VII SIXTH AND SEVENTH LESSONS   94

Perfecting the seat at the sitting trot by moving with the horse. Sitting trot with the toes hanging naturally. Suppling exercises at the sitting trot. The seat at the canter. "To go to the right, prevent the horse from going to the left." Elastic compression. Control through intermittent actions of the aids.

VIII EIGHTH LESSON   103

Sitting trot and canter. Moving with the horse at the canter. Weighting the left side facilitates the strike-off into a canter on the right lead.

IX NINTH LESSON   106

Sitting trot. Canter without stirrups, the toes raised. Jumping "without reins." Turning at the canter (supporting rein).

X TENTH LESSON   110

Rhythmic suppling exercises at the canter. Rhythmic action of the legs and play of the elbows at the canter. The gallop in supple suspension. Jumping series of cavaletti without reins. Striking off into a canter. Halting from a canter. Backing.

XI THE GAITS   115

XII "RATIONAL JUMPING"   120

XIII FURTHER IMPROVEMENT   122

Basic Equitation

General Reflections on Riding and Horses

I. Riding

Admittedly, all sports develop our physical qualities—our agility, skill, strength and stamina. Many of them also develop, to a greater or lesser degree, our moral qualities as well. But of all sports, it is riding which unquestionably develops all of these qualities most harmoniously, and which influences most favorably the development of the whole man.

ଛ∾

In contrast to the various sports which cultivate brute strength above all, riding preserves during the physical development a precise balance between strength and suppleness. This special quality, which naturally involves moral values too, leads to more balanced and more disciplined training. Thus riding —the complete sport *par excellence*—tempers the body as it does the spirit.

Because it develops skill, agility, courage, enjoyment of risk and coolheadedness, the activity of riding affords a sense of physical power and breeds self-confidence. It also improves will-power, decisiveness, initiative and determination; and it augments the inclination and ability to dominate and obtain submission, all of which are qualities of leadership.

Training horses develops tenacity, perseverance, calmness, patience, and self-control—in short, all of the qualities which contrast with anger and hot-headedness.

Moreover, riding is so fascinating that it sharpens our powers of observation and stimulates our desire to learn, both of which rapidly extend to other realms of life. It is an established fact that nobody is more interested in learning than a horseman.

Since animals, children, and all primitive creatures are subject to the same psychological laws, trainers of horses are usually skillful teachers.

The sport of riding encompasses such varied forms that it can be practised with undiminished enthusiasm until a very advanced age. Many elderly men show the same ardor in elementary or advanced dressage that they displayed in their youth on the race track or in horse shows. How grateful they feel toward riding and its essential partner, the horse, for giving them so much joy and pleasure and so many happy memories!

From the point of view of moral training, the thing that accounts for the superiority of riding is the fact that it involves the management of an animate being. It is incontestable that the companionship of animals cannot fail to enrich a person of heart and intelligence.

One who loves animals is more likely to love his neighbor also. You can never be sure that the person who shows violence or cruelty towards animals will make any distinction between them and his fellow men.

If young people only realized how delightful and worthwhile the intelligent use of the horse can be, how enthusiastically they would take up riding, instead of rushing, as they do in such numbers, to machines!

It was a happier age when speed did not exceed the natural rhythm of life. Nervous systems and ideas were certainly much better balanced than they are today.

By keeping man within the bounds of nature and its laws—which can never safely be violated—riding develops a feeling for moderation. After centuries of helping man to accelerate his locomotion, the horse now offers, in our age of rush and bustle, a useful means of slowing down.

Obviously, the engine enables us to travel faster—and faster still! But how many people, in wishing to gain a few minutes, have stupidly lost their lives! How many, caught up in the frightful whirlwind of modern life, lead a disorganized, feverish existence to the hectic and increasingly hypnotic rhythm of machines!

To guide a sensitive, living creature that is endowed with personality and initiative and which makes the efforts demanded of it with courage, cheerfulness, and willingness, is far more pleasant than it is to operate a machine. The thrill of a lively cross-country gallop on a good horse is basically very different from the sensation of driving a roaring motor over a dangerous, fume-ridden highway.

There is a considerable difference between the personalities formed by driving a car and riding a horse.

The horse accustoms you to looking far ahead and broadens your views, while the car often develops views as narrow as the thin tarred strip on which the driver must concentrate his gaze and his attention.

While cars give many people a "road hog" mentality, horses develop the "cavalier" spirit, which has always been esteemed in every field of human activity.

༄

The criticism that riders tend to be affected is quite unjustified.

Although nobody likes to admit it, everyone more or less "puts on an act" about something. Horsemen are no more affected than anyone else.

As a matter of fact, most fine riders are genuine and modest. Nothing develops modesty better than the varied and recurrent problems of training horses, and particularly of advanced dressage!

Some young Sunday riders may be conceited, but this fault will vanish as soon as their horses have had time to train them!

A phrase which was written long ago but which remains rich in truth, despite its brevity, provides an excellent conclusion for these remarks:

"L'homme se complète par le cheval"—the horse is the perfect complement to man.

II. The Horse

Since the horse and the dog are the most noble and highly developed of all animals, they deserve to be treated with respect.

The horse is not a "beast," but rather, an animal. He doesn't have a muzzle or paws; he has a mouth, limbs, and feet, just like you and me.

The horse is kindly by nature. He likes man, and submits to our commands with surprising diligence and willingness. It is usually an unskillful or brutal trainer that makes a horse become mean or vicious.

Horses are endowed with genuine intelligence, though very little thorough research has been done on this subject. We believe, however, that the difference of intelligence between horses and dogs is more a question of intellectual development than of intellectual capacity. The more closely a horse lives in contact with man, the more its intelligence develops. Perhaps if horses lived in the company of man as dogs do, instead of being relegated to the stable, they would demonstrate in just a few generations an intelligence equal to the dog's.

Horses are capable of thinking. When a rider wishes to teach a new dressage movement, for example, it often happens that his horse eagerly performs on the next day the very movement his rider was demanding the day before.

Horses also possess judgment. They know perfectly well when they are misbehaving. It is quite common to see a horse wait until the groom turns his back before doing something naughty, or for a loose horse to dash back into its stall when it hears somebody coming, only to sneak out again as soon as it is alone to resume its mischief—a quarrel with another horse, perhaps, or an extra snack stolen from tomorrow's hay.

There are many cases of horses showing likes and dislikes, both toward other horses and toward their grooms and riders.

There are also numerous examples of horses' cleverness in getting loose, by slipping their halters, or by opening doors through sliding back the bolt.

Horses are courageous. They recognize danger and are willing to face it. They may die because of it, but their courage never fails.

The thing that dominates their character the most is memory. For example, a horse that accidentally opens the riding hall gate by hitting it with his foot will do the same thing the next day, as soon as he finds himself in front of the same gate.

All the qualities we've spoken of are more highly developed in Thoroughbred horses—the aristocrats of the equine world—than in the other breeds; and they are also more highly developed in stallions and mares than in geldings.

To conclude this rapid survey, let us simply say that the horse, along with the dog, is the best and noblest friend that man has ever found.[1]

[1] It goes without saying that it is not essential to know all of this in order to learn to ride, but it is far from useless, even so. These thoughts can be expressed to pupils during rest periods, or in conversations around the stables.

Introduction

It is possible to learn to ride quickly and with little risk of falling off if the rider's training is based on rational principles and procedures.

Unfortunately, there are many riding instructors (or rather, self-styled riding instructors) who through force of habit, lack of thought or experience, or the natural tendency to reject everything that differs from what we already know, do no more than call out commands for changes of gait and direction from the center of the riding ring, and simply wait for their pupils' natural suppleness to be developed by practice.

With such methods it takes a long time for riders to acquire a seat and even then, because their legs have never been correctly positioned, the seat lacks firmness.[1]

Many riders ride badly. The cause is not exactly a lack of instructors, for there are some very good ones. It comes from the fact that anybody at all can call himself a riding instructor and give riding lessons.

Actually, of course, teaching riding is a very difficult thing which requires a great deal of experience.

[1] The seat is the factor which permits the rider to control his own balance under all circumstances.

Military regulations state that a good seat must be "supple and firm." We would prefer to say, **"firm and supple."** This is not simply a question of "six in one hand, half-a-dozen in the other." The inversion of words summarizes an important element of the method outlined in this book.

With usual methods, you wait until practice has developed the rider's suppleness sufficiently to enable him to stay on. Often this takes a long time, and a good many falls. Then, in order to help the rider to progress further and teach him to ride *correctly,* it is necessary to reposition his legs, which means a further adaptation, and loss of time.

Most riders who start this way never develop anything more than an inadequate, elementary seat, lacking the security that affords the complete mastery of the aids which is so essential to obtaining obedience and control in the right way.[2]

Only a firm seat permits the rider to advance to the second stage, and then to the advanced stages of riding, because it alone permits the rider to use his hands—and especially his legs—correctly.

How many riders stay at an elementary level because their seat is not secure enough to let them use their legs, which must replace the hands more and more as the rider gradually progresses!

Since only the correct adjustment of the legs can give the rider a firm seat and absolute control of his aids, there is no reason for the novice rider not to learn, from the very beginning, the means that provide the greatest security on horseback: engaging the

---

[2] "Aids" are what the rider uses to control the horse: legs, hands, and upper body. These are the "natural aids." The riding crop, for example, is an "artificial aid."

calves below the thickest part of the horse's oval body.[3]

By starting with a correct leg placement, the rider is given solidity and security of the seat; he is practically anchored onto the horse, as it were, so that he cannot fall off. Thus he rapidly gains confidence, his suppleness develops even more quickly, and as soon as he has acquired an adequate seat, he is ready to progress toward advanced equitation.

A good seat consists of **adherence** by the largest possible area of contacting surfaces (which is the principal element of security) and **suppleness** of the joints.

This is why we said that the seat should be **"firm and supple." First firmness, and then suppleness.**

Such a seat permits the rider to control his balance under all circumstances and to follow the horse's movements; at the same time it provides him with the necessary security and freedom for employing his aids with maximum freedom, independence, precision, tact, and clarity.

※

This book is the result of many years' experience in the instruction, study, and observation of riding. It is based on the modern rational seat which has been used by all the riders trained at Saumur since Colonel Danloux was *Écuyer en Chef*. These rational concepts are principally distinguished by the fact that **engaging the calves below the thickest part of**

---

[3] The legs are said to be correctly adjusted or positioned "when they have the maximum area of contact with the horse" (Baucher) and this contact remains constant.

the horse's body constitutes the most effective means of staying on for the rider.[4]

This book will permit horsemen who have started badly or who simply ride in some instinctive, natural way, to at last leave the stage at which they're stuck and progress toward advanced equitation, while working by themselves.

It can also serve as a guide for the many riding instructors whose only knowledge consists of vague memories of old-fashioned military regulations, and who are content to teach riding in the same way they were taught, using principles dating from 1900, a period when military concepts of riding were on the wrong track.

By adopting the method and the proven procedures that are described within these pages, the young rider is certain to make rapid progress. With the risk of falling off very much reduced, he will learn to ride with the correctness, tact, and elegance which characterize French riding at its most classical.

---

[4] For a further discussion of these concepts, see *"Equitation Raisonée," "Instruction Equestre"* and *"Evolutions Equestres"* by the same author.

In order to facilitate the study and review of the lessons in this book, everything concerned with the control of the horse is printed in ***italics***.

Illustrator's note: The rider's positions and actions have been purposely exaggerated in the drawings, in order to emphasize the points described in the text.

CHAPTER I

The Beginner's Reflexes

The natural reflexes of a person on horseback are all wrong.

It is useful to recognize what they are in order to suppress them and to develop sound reflexes right from the very beginning.

Since only thinking can substitute good reflexes for bad ones, the riding instructor should give his students logical explanations and appeal to their intelligence. This clearly requires a knowledge which can only be acquired by personal effort, broad experience, and the study of the works of those who have mastered the subject.

Little by little, the pupil's conscious acts will be transformed, through repetition of exercises and force of habit, into unconscious actions. When the reflexes of the pedestrian have been replaced by those of a horseman, he will be trained.

For the moment, we will only mention briefly the reflexes which must be fought. More detailed explanations of these reflexes and procedures for combatting them will be given later.

The novice rider always tends (compare figs. 1 and 2):

—to sit too far back in the saddle—instead of sit-

Fig. 1. The beginner's instinctive position.

Fig. 2. A good position.

ting as far forward as possible and holding his back as if he were standing up instead of sitting down;

—**to throw his shoulders forward**—instead of holding his upper body erect so that it is balanced on the seatbones;

—**to place his legs too far forward and to press down on the stirrups**—instead of bending his knees and pushing his heels back under his buttocks, without pressing on the stirrups;

—**to lower his head**—causing his loins to round, instead of keeping his line of vision parallel with the ground so that he can keep his back in its natural posture.

So much for the rider's "position," which applies, it should be emphasized, only when his horse is standing still. As soon as the horse moves, it is no longer the rider's "position," strictly speaking, that must be considered, but his coordination of movement. **The seat is inseparable from the idea of movement.**

ತಿ⇒

When the horse is moving, the novice rider tends, in addition to the bad reflexes already mentioned:

—**to be rigid**—when he should, on the contrary, move **with** the horse. Trying to remain rigid on something that's moving makes you feel the jolts even more. The only way to keep your balance on a moving support and accompany its movements is by making movements which blend with those you wish to minimize;

—**to hang onto the reins**—when the correct way to avoid falling off is by using the equilibrium of the upper body without the help of the hands, and if necessary, by engaging the legs (figs. 3, 4, 5, and 6).

Fig. 3. The seat at the walk (reins intentionally loose).

Fig. 4. The seat at the posting trot (reins intentionally loose).

Fig. 5. The seat at the sitting trot (reins intentionally loose).

Fig. 6. The seat at the canter (reins intentionally loose).

CHAPTER II

First Lesson

SUMMARY: I. What you should know before mounting: Safety warnings; saddling, bridling, leading the horse. II. To horse! Mounting and dismounting. The rider's adjustment: enveloping with the legs. The horse's line of equilibrium. The balance of the upper body. How to use your legs and hands. Feeling the rhythm of the horse's neck movements and the horse's mouth. The halt. Principal suppling exercises.

I. What you should know before mounting.

The first things to tell a novice rider are some words of caution. They can serve for his whole riding career and still not diminish the taste for excitement which every rider should possess.

Horses are most dangerous when you are standing close to them; when you are mounted you are infinitely safer. Beware of kicks. Even the steadiest horse, one you have known for a long time, could always kick through fear (as a defense reflex), because it is irritated by flies or heat, or even, perhaps, because it was struck by a rough or clumsy groom a few minutes earlier. Be especially careful with mares, for they are often somewhat lunatic.

The horse's ears ("the rider's barometer," as they have been called) can tell you about its state of mind. Their movements give the horse extremely varied expressions. When a horse lays its ears back, it feels mean (fig. 7); when the ears are pushed forward, it is afraid (fig. 8); flicking the ears in all directions is a sign of uneasiness.

After giving these words of warning, have the beginner saddle his horse in its stall. He will thus learn

Fig. 7. Look out—he wants to nip!

Fig. 8. Look out for shying!

to warn the horse of his approach before entering the stall, and to put on the saddle and bridle himself, which every rider should know how to do.

The instructor can use this opportunity to rapidly review the names of the different parts of the horse and the saddle: the horse's forehand, haunches, croup, hocks, withers, etc.; the cantle and the pommel of the saddle, its panels, girth, skirts, flaps, seat, stirrups, etc.

Then the pupil should bridle the horse, learning the adjustment and terminology of the different parts of the bridle: the browband, snaffle, curb, throatlatch, etc.

Next, while going to the riding ring, he will learn how to lead a horse (fig. 9). The reins should be separated by the index finger and grasped in the right hand about 6 inches from the horse's mouth, with the fingernails toward the ground; the hand held high and firmly, if the horse is not perfectly

Fig. 9. Leading the horse.

quiet; the ends of the reins in the left hand. Never look at the horse in order to make it move forward —this will only have the opposite effect. If another horse is in front of you, stay a safe distance behind in order to avoid being kicked. Walk ahead of your horse, or at its shoulder; as soon as you get behind the horse's shoulder you are in a dangerous position, for the horse can turn away, swing its quarters toward you, and let go with its heels. **The farther you are from the horse you are leading, the greater your risk of being kicked.** If the horse resists or tries to pull away, hold the reins very firmly in the right hand. Letting go with the right hand and being dragged at the end of the reins by a horse that is trying to pull away is very dangerous. The horse gradually gains ground, and when it has managed to get ahead of you, it can usually snatch the reins away by shying (fig. 10).

Give full importance, my young riding friends, to these safety warnings. Take as many risks as you like

Fig. 10. A dangerous way of leading.

when you are on the horse's back, but don't expose yourself to stupid accidents when you are on foot beside it. Beware of kicks! They're not all fatal, of course—luckily!—but they can be very dangerous.

When the rider has reached the center of the riding ring, he slips the reins over the horse's head.

The rider should be taught to acquire the habit of checking, with a rapid glance, the adjustment of the saddle and bridle before mounting. The mouthpiece of the bit should touch the corners of the horse's lips without wrinkling them; the browband should be in place, the throat latch loose enough to hold a fist; the saddle should be correctly placed with the sweat flaps lying flat. Check the girth, and adjust the stirrup leathers by measuring them against your arm.[1] Before doing all of this, slip your arm through the reins to prevent the horse from moving away (figs. 11 and 12). Afterwards, the rider moves to the left side of the horse, which is also called the mounting side or "near side." (The right side of the horse is called the "off side".) Finally he checks and adjusts his own clothing. **Riding and sloppiness don't mix.**

II. To horse!

The instructor shows the rider how to mount and dismount.

To mount (figs. 13, 14, 15): Stand at the horse's left shoulder. Place the left hand, in which the reins are held flat, on top of the horse's neck, while the right hand holds the ends of the reins. Keeping the reins in the left hand, drop the free end over the right side of the horse's neck. Face the stirrup. Place your left foot all the way in the stirrup, assisting with the right hand if necessary. Move closer to the horse in such a way that the *inside* of your left knee is against the saddle. Place your right hand behind the pommel. Raise yourself by springing from the right leg and lightly pulling yourself up with your arms, while keeping the left knee against the saddle and leaning the trunk forward in order to prevent the saddle from turning. Stand in the left stirrup; swing your right leg over the horse's croup, and lower yourself gently to the saddle (fig. 15). Take one rein in each hand and slip the right foot into the stirrup. Be sure to avoid jabbing the horse's flank with the

[1] When the leathers are measured against the rider's outstretched arm with the tips of the fingers touching the stirrup-bar, the sole of the stirrup should reach the armpit.

Fig. 11. What you shouldn't do.

Fig. 12. How to do it.

Figs. 13, 14 and 15. Mounting.

tip of the left foot while mounting, for this could make a touchy horse move at the very moment you are about to swing up.

To Dismount: Take both reins in the left hand and place it on top of the horse's neck. Slip your right foot out of the stirrup and place your right hand on the pommel. Stand in the left stirrup and swing your right leg, the knee slightly bent, over the horse's croup without touching it; bring the right foot close to the left one, leaning the trunk a little forward (fig. 16). Lower yourself lightly to the ground while supporting yourself on the left hand, so that you land close to the horse's shoulder, facing the rear—in other words, in the position from which you prepared to mount (fig. 17).

By mounting and dismounting in this way, the rider is always in control of his horse and always out of range of the horse's hoofs.

After a demonstration by the instructor, the pupil himself is asked to mount.

ఌ

Man was not designed by nature for horseback riding. His anatomy does not readily permit his legs to encompass the cylindrical shape of the horse's body, and his normal suppleness is insufficient to absorb the concussion of the horse's locomotion. **An effort of adaptation is therefore necessary** in order to learn to ride.

This adaptation involves, in particular, the rider's need to encircle the horse's oval body with his legs. The logical way to pick up a round object is to grasp it below its diameter and not above. Gripping with the knees above the diameter of the horse's body has a tendency to push the rider out of the saddle; it

Figs. 16 and 17. Dismounting

also deprives his knees of flexibility, for a gripping knee is necessarily a stiff one. Nevertheless, the rider must be able to stick on when he needs to (and at the beginning the need is frequent); if he cannot hang on with his calves, he will do so with his hands. This should obviously be avoided, because he needs the freedom of his hands in order to control the horse, and also must avoid hindering the movements of its neck (which is the principal balancing factor in its locomotion).

It is the grip of the calves below the diameter of the horse's body that provides the rider with the most effective means of staying on (fig. 18).

In order to encompass—or we might say, "girdle" —the horse's body with his legs, the rider must bend his knees and make a torsion at the ankles, while raising his toes as if he wished to look at the soles of his boots (figs. 18 and 19). This torsion of the ankles

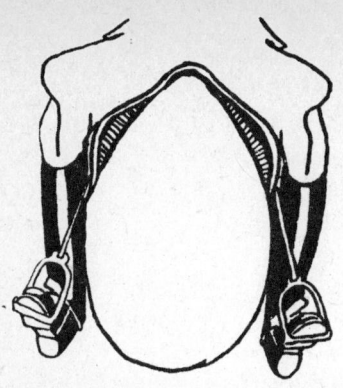 

Fig. 18. Calves engaged below the diameter of the horse's body.

Fig. 19. The torsion of the lower leg enables the legs to envelop the horse's body.

brings the lower part of the leg close to the horse's body and at the same time leaves the knee in contact with the saddle, without squeezing. The instructor, standing on the mounting side, can take the pupil's heel in his right hand, the sole in his left hand, and press the rider's calf against the curve of the horse's side behind the girth, in order to let him feel the direction his own efforts should take (fig. 20).[2]

Pressing on the big toe will bring the lower part of the leg closer to the horse. In order for this pressing to be effective, the tread of the stirrup irons must be at right angles to the horse's body.

By pressing his left hand on the rider's flexed knee while holding his right hand underneath the foot in the stirrup, the instructor can make the pupil feel

[2] The pupils should always be *made to feel* what the instructor is trying to teach them. There is a great deal of truth in the saying that in riding "to feel is to understand."

Fig. 20. The teacher makes the pupil feel the direction in which he should try.

that the more his heel is lowered, the more it locks itself under the diameter of the horse's body, and the more the lower part of the leg is pressed—almost wedged—between the curve of the horse's side and the tread of the stirrup (fig. 21).

Have the pupil increase the lowering of his heel and the pressure on the big toe by having him stand in the stirrups, so that he can feel that the lower his heels, **the knees remaining bent,** the more firmly he will be "anchored" onto the horse (fig. 22).

The lower leg cannot grip unless the calves stay in contact with the horse's sides. The pressure of the calves against the curve of the horse's sides fixes the stirrups and keeps them in place. The heels, sliding down along the curve of the sides, thus drop into a sort of corner between these two fixed points, and the lower they are, the firmer they are. Pressing on the stirrups in order to lower the heels would stiffen the leg and force the calf and stirrup away from the horse's side, destroying all the security and effectiveness of this method of setting the heels. The leg would no longer be adjusted. Pressing down on the

Fig. 21. Procedure for making pupil feel the effects of lowering the heel.

Fig. 22. The effects of lowering the heel.

stirrup while pushing the leg forward involves the risk of losing the stirrup, which cannot happen when the heels are in their correct position directly below the buttocks, with the knees bent. Be sure the rider feels this. This is why it is often preferable to ask the pupil to raise his toes, or to push his heels down and to the rear, instead of telling him to press down his heels.

Thus, **the lowering of the heels should not result from pressing on the stirrups;** quite the opposite—

the pressure on the stirrups should result from lowering the heels. The rider should try to push his calves from front to back against the curve of the horse's side and not let the pressure on the stirrups predominate, for otherwise no real security is possible. The rider would simply be "perched" on the horse and could no longer envelop it with his legs in order to stay on.

At first, the rider's knees will perhaps be carried a little away from the saddle, but this is nothing to worry about for the moment. Our aim at this point is simply the security of the rider. As his adaptation continues to improve, his knees will find their proper place against the saddle.

The torsion of the lower part of the leg clearly requires some effort at the beginning, but this is not permanent and also varies according to needs. It is obvious that a rider who is relaxing on his horse at a walk, for example, can let his legs hang naturally without any concern. For the trained rider whose muscles have been modified by exercise and practice, this holding is habitually achieved during normal movements by a simple muscular elasticity which properly speaking requires no conscious effort.[3]

Raising the toes also automatically hardens the calves, which permits the rider to communicate his energy to the horse, or in other words, to use his legs energetically; this is very important for control. Make the rider feel how slack his calves become when he raises his heels.

To get him to feel the security he acquires by en-

---

[3] We had special "offset" stirrups made at Saumur some years ago which enjoyed a certain vogue at the time; by automatically producing this torsion of the leg, they adapt the rider automatically. These stirrups are still manufactured.

gaging the calves under the diameter of the horse's body, ask the rider to squeeze with his knees, and push him sideways. He will feel how insecure he is. Then he should be asked to engage his calves while he is pushed again; he will feel the difference immediately.

The rider can be made to feel his security in another plane through the same process. As he stands in the stirrups and stretches both arms forward, the instructor presses his calves behind the girth, against the curve of the horse's side. The support of the calves will permit him to hold himself in this position. If he grips with his knees, however, he will lose his balance and fall forward (fig. 23).[4]

Once the rider has understood these basic principles, place him in the saddle.

Whether he is on foot or on horseback, man's balance depends on the position of his feet. On foot, the truth of this is obvious. In order to remain in balance, the shoulders must be in line with the heels.

Show this to the rider by making a "bridge" through drawing the shoulders back (fig. 24). It is the same in riding. Staying on a horse, like staying on one's feet, is a question of balance. It is therefore important to **make the rider feel** his "line of equilibrium" on horseback, the vertical line on which he will more or less "slide" in order to make the posting trot comfortable and to ensure the most efficient exploitation of the horse's energy; it is also along this line that the rider will hold himself in supple suspension when galloping cross-country (while hunting, for example) or in order to spare the horse

---

[4] This demonstration is so to the point that it will permit you to refute, without discussion and waste of time, all objections and contrary opinions.

Fig. 23. Results of supporting the calf against the curve of the horse's side.

Fig. 24. Balance of a man on foot.

the burden of his body weight when landing after a jump (figs. 25, 26, 27).

Take the rider's calf in the left hand and set it in its proper place behind the girth against the horse's side. Have the rider rise out of the saddle with his trunk erect and his chin forward. Support the small of his back with the right hand (fig. 28), and then ask him to lower himself into the saddle, still keeping **the trunk erect,** by letting his knees slide forward while his back remains in its natural posture, that is to say, well supported and slightly arched. If the movement has been performed correctly, the rider should come down on the pommel. Since he cannot very well sit on the pommel, he should place himself in the saddle as close to it as possible, in other words, **as far forward as possible** (fig. 29). All the great teachers have advised sitting in the saddle "as far forward as possible"—("leaving a hand's width," as La Guérinière specified, "between the buttocks and the cantle"). The closer the rider sits to the horse's with-

Figs. 25 and 26. The rider's line of equilibrium at the posting trot, and at the gallop in supple suspension.

Fig. 27. Line of equilibrium of the rider in jumping (landing phase).

ers—the axis of its movements—the less he will feel the concussion.

Because one cannot stay right on the pommel, the line of equilibrium on horseback passes slightly in front of the rider's nose (fig. 29). This is why the rider must lean the upper part of his body slightly

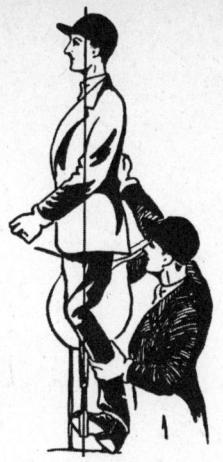

Fig. 28. Placing the rider in the saddle.

Fig. 29. The rider in place.

forward during the posting trot in order to "slide" along the line of equilibrium.

Once the rider has been placed correctly in the saddle, have him slide his heels back underneath the buttocks. The rider should find himself more or less over his heels (fig. 29). He can thus easily push himself up out of the saddle, support his pelvis with his heels, and place himself without effort in supple suspension (as at the posting trot, gallop, and during jumping). Besides, the upward pressure of his calves below the diameter of the horse's body, which is possible when the rider is properly adjusted and suitably mounted, tends to increase the pressure of the buttocks on the saddle, and consequently to increase the rider's adherence.

&

The rider's security on horseback depends on his adherence. This, in turn, depends not only on the extent of the surfaces in contact, but also on the **pressure** on these surfaces.

How can the rider increase the pressure of his buttocks on the saddle? Principally, by the weight of his trunk. During riding instruction, it is necessary to constantly keep in mind the idea of **equilibrium**. The instructor's riding crop can be balanced on his hand because every part of it rests on the part below, down to the end which rests on his hand. It is the same with the rider's trunk. In order for the trunk to remain erect and to increase the pressure of the buttocks on the saddle, the rider must raise his head, arch his trunk, draw back his shoulders—"with the back flat behind," requested La Guérinière, "and a slight hollow between the shoulders." In this posture, an erect upper body will increase the pressure of the buttocks on the saddle (fig. 30).

Fig. 30. The erectness of the upper body increases the pressure and adherence of the buttocks.

This is why one cannot be a good rider without being a graceful one. To look graceful you must raise your head, expand your chest, and keep your trunk erect. **To be a good rider, you must stay on the horse through the erectness and balance of the trunk.**

In this posture, the rider will be balanced **on his seatbones** (the ischions) and not on his thighs. In order to make the pupil feel this balance on the seatbones, ask him to separate and slightly raise his thighs, to hold them in this position and then to try to find his balance by bending the trunk **slightly** backward, only as far as necessary in order to find his balance. The rider can then return his heels to their proper position without disturbing the balance of his trunk.

Thus the joint effect of the erectness of the trunk and the weight of the **flexed legs** is to increase the pressure of the seatbones on the saddle and consequently to increase the rider's adherence and stability.

The rider's loins should remain in their natural position, that is to say, slightly curved; they are thus **prepared to act in flexion or extension as the horse's movements may require.** A rider should therefore never simply "sit" in the saddle except, of course, when he wants to be a passenger. But as soon as he wishes to work or control his horse he must, in effect, "stand up." Xenophon, who was a great horseman, was the first to say: "You must ride a horse as if you were standing up with your legs apart" (figs. 31, 32).

Fig. 31. A poor position of the loins.
Fig. 32. A good position.

The direction of the rider's vision is very important. He should look far ahead, and his line of sight should always be parallel to the ground. Looking down at the ground lowers the head and leads to a rounding of the back and a loss of balance forward (fig. 31). Looking far ahead produces the opposite effects, and helps to preserve the rider's equilibrium (figs. 32, 33).

Fig. 33. You ride like this . . . . . not like this.

Now at last the rider should have a clear conception of the correct "position" on horseback.[5] But before having him move off, give him the first essential ideas about control:

In order to control the horse, the rider has at his

---

[5] The first part of the lesson may advantageously be given on a wooden horse. This procedure keeps the pupil more attentive, since he does not have to worry about a live animal, and it also spares the horse unnecessary fatigue. In this case, of course, the rider starts off on a wooden horse, and only afterwards learns to saddle, bridle, and to lead the horse to the ring.

disposal **an accelerator** (*his legs*) and **a brake** (*the bit*).

*How to use the legs: Once the rider's legs have been correctly placed and "adjusted," if he wishes his horse to move forward, increase the speed, or go into a faster gait, he gradually increases the even pressure of his calves, squeezing more and more strongly until the horse responds. If this action proves to be insufficient, and **only then**, he can use varying pressure of the calves. If this is still insufficient, he can kick with the calves, then with the heels.*

The rider should acquire the habit of acting progressively in this way. This will teach him to adjust his actions to the horse's sensitivity, and will develop his muscles and the "squeeze" of his calves. Too many riders confine their leg actions to kicking, and since they usually fail to yield with their hands at the same time, they have difficulty in controlling the horse.

The heels should always be used with vigor and energy. **The horse must respect the rider's legs.** *It is the legs, later reinforced by the spurs, which discipline the horse and compel it to obey.*

Horses are like children and all primitive creatures in that only strong stimuli make a deep and permanent impression on them. **Strong stimuli also have the great advantage of not requiring frequent repetition.** *If the horse is to respect the rider's legs, they must never make any half-hearted, flabby actions to which the horse would soon become accustomed and which would eventually cause it to ignore the rider's legs. If the horse does not obey the action of the calves, attack with the heels, always in a very energetic and authoritative manner. Like steering a boat or driving a car, riding a horse **depends on for-***

ward movement, that is to say, on the horse's response to the rider's legs.

From the very first lessons, this idea of the necessity of forward movement must be impressed upon the rider. Most riders use their hands much too much, and their legs not enough.

The place where the rider's leg actions are applied is no casual matter. Too many riders think that the further back their legs are applied, the stronger their effect will be; this is untrue. In order to produce a maximum effect on the horse's impulsion, the leg must act close to the girth.[6]

How to use the hands: On horseback as in a car, you should never start to move while the brake is on. But, since you must be able to use the brake at any time, it is important to establish an elastic, **constant** support with the horse's mouth, as if the reins were a very fine elastic ribbon which you wished to keep constantly stretched without breaking.

The rider should realize that, by means of the reins and bit, he is in contact with the horse's tongue, the corners of its lips, and the "bars," that is, its gums. He should take care never to harm these areas, which are highly sensitive, and **never abuse the horse with the hands.**

Continual pressure on the bit results, through a tourniquet effect, in cutting off the circulation and consequently in numbing the horse's mouth. One can easily verify that the tongue of a horse ridden by a heavy-handed rider who hangs onto the reins will quickly turn blue or even violet.

In order to use the hands correctly, you must **never**

---

[6] Near to the point of attachment of the abdominal muscles. See *"Equitation Raisonée"* by the same author.

pull on the reins. This is not mere theory; it is what you must always put into practice.

*Why should you never pull on the reins? Because, **if you pull on the reins, the horse will pull the opposite way**—it is a physiological, mechanical, normal, natural reaction. If you are standing in front of me and I push you with my hand, what do you do in order to avoid falling? You push forward. If I stand behind you and pull you backwards, you will pull in the opposite direction. The horse reacts in exactly the same way:*

"Action = Reaction"

*This can also be expressed by saying that **there are no horses who are pullers, but only riders who pull**. There are no hard-mouthed horses, there are only heavy-handed riders. We are always tempted, unjustly, to blame the horse.*

*The reins are pulled only in special cases. The racing jockey, for example, who wants his horse to extend itself, pulls on the reins and the horse takes more hold. But if you do not want your horse to lean on the bit or to increase its extension, **never pull on the reins.***

*After an entire lifetime devoted to the study and practice of equitation, Baucher, the greatest horseman of all time, called to his deathbed General L'Hotte, who was himself one of our greatest riders. Closing his fingers and fixing his hand, he said, "This." Then, drawing his hand backwards, he added, "never that!" Heed the words of a master: "Never that!" **Never pull on your reins and you will always have pleasant, manageable horses that are easy to ride.***

Then how should you use your hands? They must

*act by **resisting**. This is accomplished by **closing the
fingers on the reins** and by setting the hands. The
rider tightens his fingers to the point of crushing the
reins if necessary, but **without drawing back his elbows the slightest bit**. His arms should be "arms of
steel," with all of their muscles set.*

*The resistance thus produced has a force that is
infinitely more convincing to the horse than pulling. **Through resistance, you will overcome all resistance in the horse. By pulling, you only provoke
resistance.***

*It is obvious that in order for the horse to feel the
resistance of the fingers, **the reins must be the right
length**. The instructor can have the pupil feel this
by resisting against poorly adjusted reins, and then
against properly adjusted ones (fig. 34).*

*At the beginning, the rider will often attempt to
resist on reins that are not properly adjusted. In order
to halt the horse, for example, if the horse does not
obey at first, he should shorten the reins and repeat
the action (fig. 35).*

*In any case, the pupils should acquire from the
start the habit of **not persisting in the use of methods
which do not produce obedience immediately**. If the
horse does not obey, shorten the reins and start again
—or try something else.*

*The instructor should insist on the fact that **the
resistance of fixed hands is possible only if the rider
tightens his fingers on the reins. If he does not
tighten the fingers, he will be inclined to pull**.*

*As he talks, the instructor demonstrates how the
reins should be held between the thumb and index
fingers, with the other fingers acting as a spring.*

*One final demonstration before having the rider
move his horse forward:*

Fig. 34. For the horse to feel your resistance, the reins must be adjusted. (Note that the instructor, in order to make the resistance, must take a braced stance.)

Fig. 35. To avoid having to shorten the reins, a rider with an adequate seat can raise his hands, but always without withdrawing his elbows at all from front to back.

Tell him to hold the reins firmly. The instructor then stands in front of the horse with his shoulder underneath the horse's neck; he grasps one rein in each hand and pulls on them. The rider is easily pulled forward (fig. 36). Now ask the rider to arch his

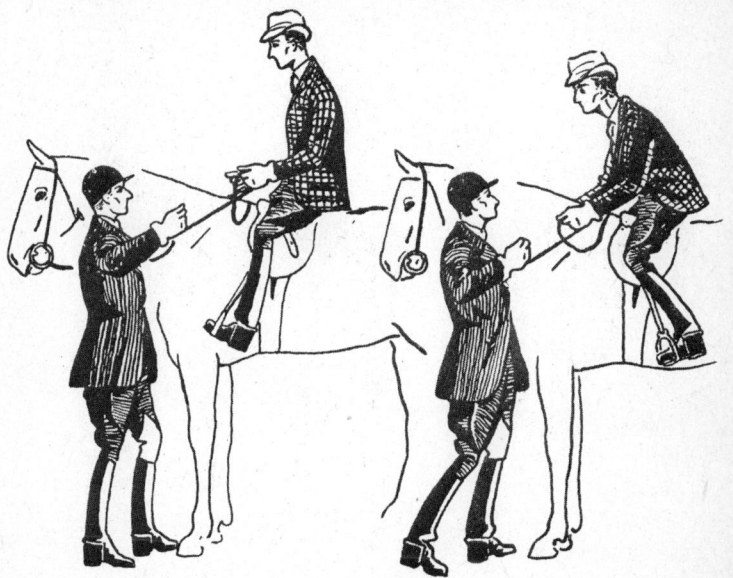

Fig. 36. *Demonstrating the necessity of a firm foundation to support resistance.*

loins and to stretch his trunk up. Repeat the pulling process. The rider will feel that in these conditions, he is able to resist the instructor's pulling (fig. 37). He will then understand that **in order to produce distinct resistance which the horse cannot possibly confuse with pulling, the resistance must be supported from the firm base of the pelvis.** *This firm base is established by stretching the trunk upwards with the small* of the back supported. *The stiffened spinal column is more or less braced against the pommel* (fig. 37). *If the rider acts in this way to halt, for example,* **bringing his hips closer to his wrists,** *and not the wrists to*

Fig. 37. Resistance must be supported from the firm base of the pelvis.

the hips, and setting his hands as if the wrists were bolted to the saddle, he becomes a sort of fixed mechanism. The thing that makes such devices useful is their automatic operation. The disobedient horse provides its own punishment. It hurts itself, and it is not the rider who hurts it. There is a great difference.

On foot as on horseback, you cannot resist a pull unless you have first braced yourself. Unless you do so on horseback, you are subject to the full force *of the traction and can only defend by pulling (figs. 36, 37).*

Therefore, when the rider wishes to impose his will on the horse, to stop it or control it, he must act:

1) **with the back** *(through which the rider creates a firm base from which to support the resisting action of the fingers).*

2) **with the hands** *(arms of steel,* **closed fingers,** *without the slightest withdrawal of the elbows) (fig. 37).*

❧

While these demonstrations will require a certain amount of time, it is by no means time wasted. Even so, some people will no doubt think that this first lesson is too theoretical.

Every method has some advantages and drawbacks. As far as we are concerned, however, we firmly endorse this method of proceeding, for we have used it for a long time and it proves its effectiveness anew every day.

It is extremely important, we believe, to get a good start in riding. It is the first two or three lessons which establish the basic style and sound principles on which everything else will depend. This is why we think it necessary to take such great pains with these first fundamental lessons, which provide a firm and solid foundation for subsequent training.

It is important for the rider to be perfectly clear from the beginning about the best way to get on and stay on a horse, and to possess from the very start a clear and precise idea of how the aids should be used. It is necessary to spend just as much time as this requires. We must look beyond the first lesson. And what may, perhaps, be considered lost time for the first lesson itself is unquestionably time gained for all the lessons that follow.

※

Now the rider can start to move at a walk. In order to initiate forward motion, the horse must shift its weight forward, just as we do. It does this by stretching out its neck. The rider must allow the neck the extension which his legs demand by stretching his arms forward.

"*Forward.*" "*Tighten your calves and give your horse its head. Push it forward by yielding with your hands and extending your arms, without depriving the horse of the support of the reins.*"

Ask the rider to observe the horse as it walks.

It moves its neck, which serves as a counter-balance, just as we swing our arms when we walk. The horse uses its neck in this way during the walk and the canter. It holds its neck in a fixed position only when trotting. Consequently, **only at the trot should the rider keep his hands immobile.** *At the walk and canter they must move, in order not to hinder the horse's neck movements and its locomotion. A horse might be compared to a clock, which works only when the pendulum is swinging. In order to "work," the horse also requires the free movements of its pendulum. The rider should therefore not set himself in a fixed position; he should, on the contrary, capture the feeling of the rhythm of the horse's movements and try not to interfere with them.*

Contagiously or by contact, the rider communicates to the horse all of his proclivities: his mobility, his inertia, his suppleness, his stiffness, his tension, his energy, his weakness, his activity, his nonchalance, etc. "If you wish your horse to **walk,** *rather than to* *creep and drag along the way it is doing, move, move **with** your horse. Communicate to it your activity and mobility."*

*During the walk, the rider should try to catch the feeling of the rhythm of the horse's neck movements by relaxing his elbows and trying to establish a supple, soft, elastic and **constant** contact with the horse's mouth.*

*In order to establish such a contact, **the horse must carry its own head, and the rider must carry his own hands.** The rider should not make the horse carry his hands, nor should the horse make the rider carry its head. Both of them should remain independent. When this is so, the rider, being the more intelligent one, should create by the play of his elbows the supple and constant connection that must exist between the horse and him. **The rider must try to make the horse feel the elasticity of his elbows and not the weight of his hands.** Then the horse, confident in the rider's hands, will "yield its head" and submit to the rider.*

*In order for the rider to be able to carry his hands, he must hold them with the **thumbs up.** Thus, the forearm can be carried by the upper arm, which hangs down straight (figs. 38, 39).[7]*

Ask the rider to walk on while counting: "one, two, one, two," moving his hands slightly forward every time the horse extends its neck at the count of "one" or "two."

Correct the way the rider holds the reins and the position of his hands as often as necessary.

---

[7] Asking the rider to "hold the elbows close to the body" would tend to immobilize his hands. But if his thumbs are up, his elbows will naturally be in the proper position with the springs of the elbow joints well set to operate effectively.

Fig. 38. To be able to carry his own hands, the rider must keep his thumbs up.

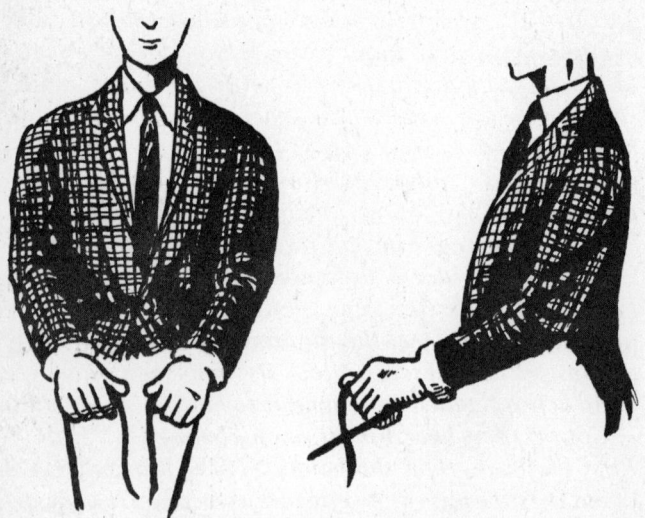

Fig. 39. Incorrect holding of the reins—the rider makes the horse carry the weight of his hands.

*The hands should not be held too close together. There should be **at least** the width of the bit between them.*

Let the rider practice feeling the rhythm of the neck movements while counting. See that he keeps his trunk erect and his toes raised.

The accompanying movement of the hands is not a perfectly regular backward and forward movement; since the horse's movement of lowering its neck is shorter than the movement of raising it, the forward movement of the rider's hands should be more rapid than their backward movement, which should be slower, as if it were restrained.

When the rider has begun to feel the cadence of the neck movements, he can be taught to halt.

*While having him continue at a walk, remind him of what he should do in order to halt: "When I tell you to halt, you will make yourself immobile, and communicate your immobility to your horse by contact. You will act at first: 1) **with the back**, taking care not to draw the elbows back, but bringing your hips up closer to your hands; then 2) **with the hands, tightening the fingers** and immobilizing the hands (arms of steel)."*

Before having him perform these actions, make sure that the rider is accompanying the horse's neck movements with the play of his elbows, so that the horse will clearly feel the difference between the hand actions which merely follow its movement and the hand actions which command it to halt.

Count, then have him stop on command: "Halt!— First the back, then the hands." If the horse does not obey, it is because the reins are too long. If they are much too long, have him shorten them and begin again. If they are only slightly too long: "Don't pull!

Raise your hands." If the horse still does not stop, it is because the rider is pulling.

The stretching of the rider's trunk should be performed with smooth coordination, and the movement should relate to the muscular activity of the horse which the rider wishes to control.

In order to develop the horse's obedience, it is important to be alert to the first sign of obedience so that you can "yield as soon as the horse yields," and **decrease the intensity of your command as soon as the horse has started to obey.**

Practice the halt until it is well performed.

This is how a well-trained rider proceeds: he controls his horse by controlling its neck movements. First of all, he smoothly follows the movements he wishes to control. Then if he wishes to extend the gait, he drives with his legs while his elbows accentuate the extending movements of the horse's neck. He diminishes these actions if he wishes the horse to slow down. He stops them if he wishes the horse to halt.[8]

The rider will be surprised by the ease with which he can bring a horse to a halt if he follows these instructions. Respond to his surprise by explaining that the horse is capable of obeying signals which are infinitely finer still, more delicate than he could possibly imagine.

No act of force should ever be made by the hands. ***It is always abuse by the hand that provokes resistance and defenses.***

During the last fifteen minutes or so of the lesson,

---

[8] Since the horse's neck does not swing during the trot, at this gait the resistance of the fingers *on adjusted reins* with fixed hands will suffice.

teach the rider the most useful exercises for combatting bad reflexes and developing the seat:

—Have him drop his stirrups, and then practice:

—Suppling the extremities: rotating the head, the wrists, the feet.

—Rotating the arms, the shoulders, and the trunk, with the arms held horizontally.

—Flexing the knees.

—Patting the right side of the horse's croup with the left hand, and the left side with the right hand, **while arching the back and trying to lower the knees.**

—Then, with one hand held behind the back with the palm facing outwards, practice moving **the small of the back** by giving a series of short pushes against the belt buckle, while throwing the shoulders back in order to increase the freedom of action of the back, pulling the trunk up tall in cadence with the rhythm of the horse's walking movements. At the same time, practice moving the hand which holds the reins and the legs, keeping the knees supple, in cadence with the walking steps.

This first time, the instructor should not be too particular about the absolute correctness of these movements. They will be studied more closely during the following lesson.

Now at rest, the rider holds the ends of the reins at the buckle.

Finally, he dismounts. The reins are passed over the horse's head and it is led back to the stable. "Hold on to the reins, and beware of kicks!"

CHAPTER III

Second Lesson

SUMMARY: Suppling exercises. Contact with the horse's mouth. Halts. The trot in supple suspension and the posting trot. The sitting trot, raising the toes.

After the rider has led his horse to the riding ring, have him check the adjustment of his horse's tack and of his own clothing.

When he has mounted, have him make several turns of the ring at a walk with long reins, the horse free. All lessons should start this way. During work, have him often yield the reins, in order to give the horse frequent and complete rest periods and above all, to help the rider develop the habit of **staying on the horse without the help of reins,** so that he does not continually hang on them for the whole time he is in the saddle.

Tirelessly correct bad habits.

Have him drop his stirrups and do suppling exercises.

ಆ

Suppling exercises on horseback are of great importance. Most young riders tend to neglect them.

Their purpose is to correct bad positions, to supple the rider, and to obtain and develop the independence of the different parts of his body.

Since man's natural suppleness is not sufficient to fully absorb the concussion of the horse's movement, increasing his suppleness is complementary to adapting him to the horse. It is the play and suppleness of his joints which permit the rider to follow the horse's movements, and to develop coordination.

Increasing the rider's suppleness is necessary not only for his own comfort and the horse's ease of movement, but also to enable him to preserve control over his aids despite the concussion of movement, and thus control the horse.

The jolts and bumps made by a rider who is insufficiently supple tire both horse and rider, and lead to jerks on the horse's mouth which, by hindering its movements, make propulsion uncomfortable and easy control impossible.

The independence of the aids, which otherwise may act to contradict and cancel each other, is indispensable to controlling the horse correctly.

In order for the rider to preserve the balance of his upper body on a moving horse and **maintain it with the fewest possible movements,** the rider's back must be able to act alternately and with equal facility in flexion (curved out) and in extension (stretched). There is no necessity (and indeed there are only disadvantages) in wishing to make the back work in other, unnatural ways. And since for physiological reasons the back always acts more easily in flexion, **it is primarily the extension of the back that needs to be worked on with young riders.**

Progress does not result from simply doing certain things; it depends on **how they are done.** The rider should therefore **make a real effort** to perform the prescribed suppling exercises correctly. Do not try to simplify these movements; on the contrary, increase their difficulty so that even greater effort is required.

It is important, furthermore, for the movements to be made long enough and hard enough to produce a change, an actual modification of the rider's tendons and muscles.

Seek from the start the independence of the different parts of the body. Be sure that the movements of one arm have no repercussions on the other arm or on the legs, and that the movements of one leg have no effect on the other leg, that the hands maintain contact with the horse's mouth despite the movements of the upper body, etc.

Finally, when you wish to exercise a joint—the wrist, for example—you must steady the part of the body which supports it, that is, you must immobilize the forearm. For the same reason, it is important to immobilize the leg when you wish to exercise the ankle, and try to set the pelvis if you wish to work the small of the back to the maximum.

Begin the suppling exercises with the extremities, for it is their state that determines, in general, the state of the rest of the body. When the extremities are supple, this suppleness quite naturally flows back, and little by little breaks down the rider's core of stiffness. Rotate the head, stretching the ligaments of the neck; rotate the wrists (forearm fixed); rotate the feet (by describing a circle from outside to inside with the toes, while fixing the leg and trying to raise the toes).

Next, place the rider, his trunk balanced on the seatbones, as far forward as possible in the saddle. Make him feel his equilibrium by having him **very slightly** raise his thighs, which are held away from the saddle, with the knees bent.[1]

[1] A useful way to teach the pupil to find this equilibrium of the trunk on the seatbones is to have him perform the exercise while sitting on a stool or a wooden horse (fig. 40).

This done, start with the pelvis and, going downward, supple the hips (the coxo-femoral joints). Lower the knees, taking care not to disturb the pelvis; kick the toes toward the ground.

Knee flexion: Grasp one heel with your hand and force the knee to bend while lowering the knee, engaging the pelvis, and pushing the buttocks forward (fig. 41).

Fig. 40. Procedure for feeling the sense of balance on the seatbones.

Fig. 41. Flexing the knees.

Then supple the upper part of body, starting from the pelvis: **Rotate the small of the back,** the arms held horizontally. **Stretch the loins. Rotate the arms,** bringing the shoulders back (fig. 42). **Rotate the shoulders:** Have the shoulders describe a circle from front to back, with the head held high (fig. 43). During these movements, the pupil should try to keep his heels well under the buttocks while pressing his calves against the curve of the horse's side, so that his legs girdle and envelop the horse's body.

Combine these suppling exercises by having the

Fig. 42. Arm rotation.   43. Rotation of the shoulders.

rider pat the horse on the right hip with the left hand (or the reverse) while lowering the knees and pushing the heels back and the stomach forward, **the pelvis remaining vertical over the seatbones** (fig. 44). In order to make the rider feel the direction of effort, the instructor can pull the rider's knee down and to the rear and assist the extension of the small of the back during this movement. Have the rider lean back until his head touches the horse's croup, **while trying to lower his knees and to push back his heels.**

During all these movements, the rider should make an effort to arch his back, still remaining in equilibrium and pressing down on the seatbones rather than the thighs, while **stretching** and **expanding** the front of his body, swelling his chest and trying to push his heels back into line with the shoulders (fig. 45).

Finally, the last suppling exercise: with one hand

Fig. 44. Patting the horse's left quarters with the right hand.

Fig. 45. The "arch," on a dummy horse.

behind the back, the palm facing out, push the small of the back rhythmically forward against your belt buckle while holding the shoulders back, in cadence with the movement of the walk. While counting "One, two, one, two," simultaneously move the hand holding the reins and the legs (hips and knees always supple), while pushing the heels towards the rear and down each time that the small of the back acts in extension.

These suppling exercises should be repeated at the beginning of the following lessons, and later on according to the particular weaknesses of the individual rider.

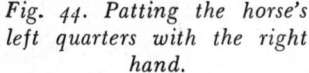

After a few minutes' rest, have the rider take his stirrups again and practice following the horse's walking movements with the play of his elbows.

The rider's hands should not be submitted to the

horse's movements; they must regulate them, and not obey them.

Extensions of gait should be achieved by seeking to accentuate the amplitude of the horse's movements rather than by accelerating the tempo.

Be careful that the rider does not bring his hands together. The contact through the reins forms a sort of corridor which the horse enters in order to move "up to the hand." In order to be responsive, the horse must be "on the aids," that is to say, "before the legs," and "on the bit." If the rider brings his wrists together, he shuts the door of the corridor, so to speak, and the horse cannot move up to the bit.

Now, a few halts, drawing the hips up to the hands, without the slightest withdrawal of the elbows. See that the upward expansion of the trunk which precedes the resistance of the fingers is performed with coordination, and not too abruptly.

Warn the rider against the common beginners' tendency, when a horse is getting away from them, to grab the pommel with both hands while still holding the reins (fig. 46). This invariably turns out badly. ***The rider must always keep the brake free.*** *Hold the pommel with one hand if necessary, but keep the reins in the other. As soon as the rider has recovered his balance he can shorten the reins, if necessary, and stop the horse (fig. 47).*

ಜ‿

Advise the pupil that if he hopelessly loses his balance, he should grab the horse's neck by wrapping both arms around it so that he can land on his feet, and protect his head and collarbone from the fall.

First exercise at the trot: The horse should be on a longe line, and the stirrup leathers should be tied

Fig. 46. This rider can't use the brake any more.
Fig. 47. Hold the pommel if you need to, but always keep the brake free.

to the girth. Attaching the stirrup leathers places the heels, establishes the rider's line of equilibrium and obliges him to bend his knees, which lessens the usual tendency of most beginners to seek an exaggerated support from the stirrups by stiffening the legs.

It is especially important during this first trotting lesson for the stirrup leathers to be correctly adjusted. To achieve this, ask the rider to envelop the horse's body as completely as possible by making a torsion of his legs while lowering the knees, raising the toes, and tightening the calves. (The calf pressure must act a little behind the girth, both rearwards—against the curve of the horse's side—and upwards, the knees being supple). The position of the soles will then indicate the correct length of the stirrup leathers.

When the foot is in the stirrup, the stirrup should be at right angles to the horse's body, facilitating the pressure of the big toe.

Have the rider rise from the saddle, not by straightening up, but with his joints (ankle, knee, and hip) slightly bent, so that they can play. Have him hold the reins in one hand and rest the other hand slightly in front of it on the horse's neck, with the palm flat and the thumb on one side of the neck and the fingers on the other, so that both hands are lightly supported by the neck. The **chin should be held forward** so that the small of the back remains arched and **the pelvis stays in the line of equilibrium** (fig. 48).

Fig. 48. The trot in supple suspension.

The purpose of the exercise is to make the rider feel the engagement of his calves below the diameter of the horse's body. Press on the stirrups as little as possible. Let the weight of the body lower the heels and push from front to back with the calves; **these must stay in place against the curve of the horse's side, legs bent,** knees supple and in the closest possible contact with the saddle **without squeezing,** the rider pressing on his big toe in order to keep the calves flat against the horse's body.

Try hard to **keep the pelvis in the line of equilibrium,** and avoid placing the shoulders too far forward.

Have the rider trot in this position; he should be more or less stretched from both ends, stretching his body up, pushing the heels backward and downward, and remaining in supple suspension along the line of equilibrium, with knees and ankles playing freely in order to absorb the concussion. The point of support of the calves will enable him to remain in balance.

When the rider performs this exercise well, and has felt the engagement of the calves underneath the diameter of the horse's body, he can be taught the posting trot. Be sure that he continues, in the posting trot, to try to engage and flex his legs and push his heels back under his buttocks, in such a way that he can easily raise the pelvis and support it as it returns to the saddle.

It is the support of the calves from front to back, against the curve of the horse's side, that the rider must use as the means of pushing his pelvis forward into the line of equilibrium; he must never pull it forward by using the reins (figs. 49 and 50).

In the posting trot, seek support from the horse's

Fig. 49. Never pull the pelvis forward with the reins ...

Fig. 50. Push it forward with the calves.

Fig. 51. Bad position at the posting trot. Shoulders too far forward.

side and limit as far as possible the support from the stirrups, which should carry only the weight of the legs.

In returning to the saddle, sit as far forward as possible. **If the rider keeps his pelvis, shoulders, and** calves correctly in the line of equilibrium, the posting trot will be produced naturally and effortlessly. Beginners often have a tendency to hold their shoulders too far forward. But **it is primarily the pelvis that must be brought forward;** the shoulders should move forward only to the degree necessary to keep them in balance in the vertical line that passes through the calves (figs. 50 and 51).

When the posting trot is done this way with the rider sliding, in effect, in supple suspension along the line of equilibrium, his ankles and knees playing, the trot is comfortable for the rider and much less tiring for the horse than if the rider squeezed with his knees. As a matter of fact, squeezing the knees hinders the forward shifting of the pelvis by limiting the play of the joints, and obliges the horse's loins and hocks to absorb the full weight of the rider's body as it returns to the saddle (figs. 52 and 53).

Balance is always balance, on foot as on horseback. The movements the rider must make at the posting

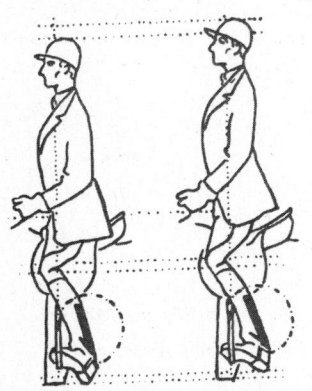

Fig. 52. Posting trot in supple suspension.

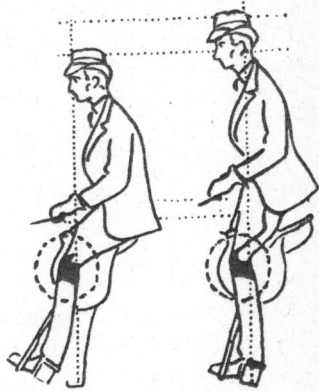

Fig. 53. Posting trot by pinching with the knees.

trot, if he wishes to stay in balance and spare his horse, are the same ones made by a man on foot who inclines his body slightly forward and does deep knee bends, rising and descending along his line of equilibrium. On horseback as on foot, this movement cannot be done in balance unless the knees and ankles play, and the pelvis remains in the same vertical as the heels.

Continue to have the rider work on the trot in supple suspension and the posting trot, with the horse off the longe line.

While taking rest breaks at a walk, frequently check the balance of the trunk by relieving weight from the thighs and stirrups.

Then hold the reins at the buckle, and drop the stirrups.

Next, a few exercises in keeping contact with the horse's mouth, and a few halts. Develop the reflex of holding the shoulders back, which is **the safety reflex for the rider.** As a practical matter, you never fall off backwards—always forward. As long as his shoulders are behind the line of equilibrium, the rider is in the safety zone; as soon as they move forward of this line, his seat becomes precarious.

The rider will become more aware of this shortly, in working at the sitting trot.

During the last fifteen minutes of the lesson, put the horse back on the longe line and continue working on the rider's adaptation by having him sit to the trot without stirrups.

Tell him to balance himself **on his seatbones** while trying to lower the knees and to push the heels down and to the rear, underneath the buttocks, the legs bent and the knees supple. He must thus envelop or girdle the horse's body with the calves while **raising the toes as much as possible.** The trunk should be stretched in such a way that the weight of the shoulders falls behind the line of the buttocks. The small of the back, thus relieved of the weight of the shoulders, will then be able to play.

The purpose of this exercise is the engagement of the calves underneath the diameter of the horse's body. This effect is possible only when the calves are hard; as soon as the toes drop, the calves become slack. The rider must be made to feel this.

Have the rider trot as described, holding onto the pommel at the beginning, stretching the front of his body, pulling the trunk up tall, and making an arch (fig. 54).

Fig. 54. The "arch" at the sitting trot.

The sitting trot is the most complete suppling exercise for putting the rider in balance and developing his seat.

When performed with toes raised and knees low-

Fig. 55. Stiffening the legs makes balance difficult.

Fig. 56. Flexing the legs facilitates balance (increasing the pressure of the buttocks).

ered, the sitting trot is the best exercise for making the seat solid and secure.[2]

ஓ≫

Continue this exercise, with the horse off the longe line.

Have the rider observe that stiffening the legs forces them forward and away from the horse's body, where their swinging movements can disturb the lateral balance. Bending the legs, on the other hand, sort of pulls in these counterweights so that their disturbing action can no longer be produced; it even facilitates the maintenance of equilibrium, since the legs, being flexed, add their own weight to the adherence of the buttocks on the saddle (figs. 55 and 56).

End the lesson with some exercises involving contact with the horse's mouth, a few halts, and finally a rest period, without stirrups and with the reins held at the buckle.

[2] The sitting trot is not invariably performed with the toes raised; it depends on the goal in view. At the beginning, we ask for raised toes because we are trying to have the rider feel the engagement of the calves that procures the most effective means of staying on, to teach him to envelop the horse's body with his calves, and to make him hold on with them so that he will not hold on with his hands.

Later on, when the rider has developed confidence and knows how to stay on and to engage his calves in case of need, he should practice the sitting trot with the toes hanging naturally. This exercise places the rider in a difficult situation and obliges him to stay on horseback exclusively by means of the suppleness of the small of the back. The sitting trot practiced in this way will thus enable the rider eventually to develop suppleness and acquire coordination.

CHAPTER IV

Third Lesson

SUMMARY: Vaulting to mount. Improving the rider's adherence at the trot in supple suspension and at the posting trot. Developing steady hands at the posting trot. Use of the reins. Improving the erectness of the trunk at the sitting trot. Regulating and directing the horse's movements. The opening rein and the indirect rein. Vaulting to dismount.

We have often had pupils who were started with the methods outlined in this book and were cantering by their third hour of lessons, without ever falling off. But one can't lay down a definite rule; one must go by the average rider. Moreover, there is no great advantage, over-all, in going too fast; it is better to follow the rider's progress than precede it. Therefore, we will not deal with the canter until the Fifth Lesson. Talented riders can start cantering earlier, as soon as they are sufficiently secure. But all pupils should be secure enough by the time they have reached the Fifth Lesson.

To vault up: Stand at the horse's withers as if you were going to mount normally, holding the shortened reins in the left hand, and putting the right hand on the pommel (fig. 57). Raise yourself on your wrists; straighten the trunk, pausing an instant in this position (fig. 58), and then place yourself lightly in the saddle.

Figs. 57 and 58. Vaulting up.

Begin the lesson with the series of suppling exercises.

Improve the rider's adherence, as described in the preceding lesson, at the trot in supple suspension and at the posting trot.

At this point, only those riders whose legs still swing need have their stirrup leathers attached to the girth.

At the posting trot, beginners have a tendency to rise too high out of the saddle, which makes them bounce. As soon as the rider understands the mechanics of this gait, advise him not to try to raise himself up, but **to let himself be lifted.** The only effort the rider has to make at the beginning is to bend his knees, in order to keep his heels underneath the buttocks and thus permit his knees and ankles to work freely. The posting trot should then be accomplished completely naturally, and without effort.

Beginners also have a tendency to let themselves go too much at the posting trot. Thus they are "taken in tow" by the horse. In order to post to the trot **with the horse**, the rider must stretch forward into the movement, more or less urging the horse forward and seeking to communicate his drive to it. In order to achieve this the rider should look straight ahead while posting, his gaze **parallel with the ground,** the trunk stretched and inclined slightly forward, the chest thrown out, the shoulders free, the small of the back supported. **It is the knees which should point forward, not the toes.**

It is through the tension of the forward gaze, the small of the back, and the calves (low heels = hard calves) that the rider transmits the drive which encourages the horse to develop impulsion energetically in the desired direction, instead of merely plodding along. As we have already said, the rider communicates to the horse, contagiously or physically, all of his moods—his passivity or energy, and his forward drive.

It is principally the free play of the rider's ankle and knee which produces coordination at the posting trot.

The legs should be supple, bent, free in the joints and not stiff. Tell the rider to relax his ankles. Call out "Heels! Heels! Heels!" in cadence with his return to the saddle at the trot. The play of the ankles will gradually spread to the knees and lend harmony to the trot.

In order for the knees and ankles to fulfill their role of shock absorbers, these joints must be in an attitude of elasticity, of controlled tension, which enables them to act like the arm of a flat spring. The ankles must not remain blocked in the fully closed position. This remark applies equally to all of the rider's joints, which must in every case play elastically, and not be locked either open or shut.

The instructor should make sure that the rider's hands remain steady at the posting trot, and do not follow the movements of the trunk up and down.

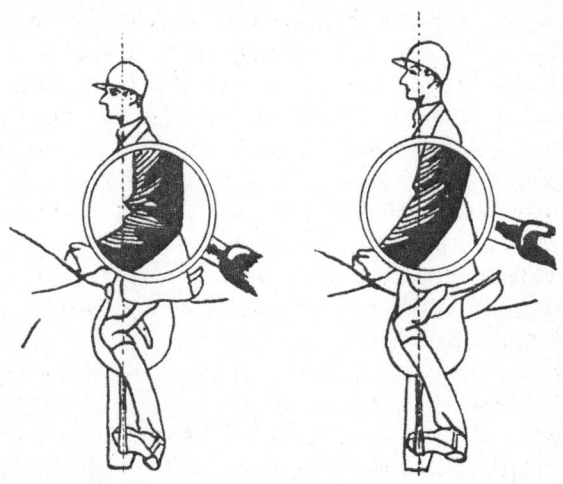

Fig. 59. Posting trot with the hands resting on the neck.

For the hands to become independent of the movements of the trunk, the elbows must play. In order to give the rider the cadence of the elbow movements, have him place his hands on the horse's neck **with the thumbs up,** so that the elbow "springs" are in position to act freely (fig. 59).

Teach the rider to trot on the left diagonal when he is on the left hand.[1]

The trotting periods should be frequent and brief. Continually adjust the rider's seat and correct bad positions. Become more and more exacting.

During rest breaks at a walk (and later at a trot, in subsequent lessons) have the rider practice dropping and recovering his stirrups and handling the reins.

Manipulating the reins is an excellent suppling exercise and accustoms the rider to being considerate of the horse's mouth.

To take **both reins in the left hand,** bring the left hand over to the middle of the body and grasp the right rein with it, separating the two reins with the little finger and letting them emerge between the thumb and the index finger. Drop the right hand to the side.

To separate the reins again, let the right hand pick up the part of the right rein held by the left hand and move the wrists ten inches apart.

The rider takes both reins in the right hand by a similar process.

In order **to shorten the reins,** the rider brings his wrists together and grasps the free end of the rein he wishes to shorten with one hand from above, near the thumb of the opposite hand.

Develop independence of the aids by holding both adjusted reins in the left hand, for example, and while maintaining soft contact with the horse's mouth with this hand, rotate the right arm, strike

[1] The rider is said to be "on the right hand" when the inside of the ring is to his right, and inversely. The rider trots on the right diagonal (on the right foot) when he resumes contact with the saddle at the moment that the horse's right forefoot touches the ground.

backward with the right fist at shoulder height, or pat the horse's right hip or left croup with the right hand.

ც~

Our purpose during this lesson is to make the rider feel the vertical alignment of his trunk at the sitting trot.

We stay on by means of the erectness and balance of the upper body. Give the rider this feeling by letting him learn what an erect upper body feels like at the sitting trot, first with stirrups and then, as soon as possible, without stirrups.

Have him correct the balance of his upper body over the seatbones at a walk (by very slightly raising the thighs). Have him perform the sitting trot while pulling on the pommel in order to engage the pelvis, with his chest thrown out, and his upper body stretched tall; then have him let go of the pommel. Next, the sitting trot without stirrups, placing one hand on the top of the croup and using this support to push the stomach forward. (Avoid twisting the back during this movement.) Draw both shoulders well back, extending the arms in order to avoid hanging on to the reins (fig. 60). Seek to align and balance the upper body over the seatbones by making an "arch"—by **stretching** and **expanding** in front, with the chest out and the back flat, while pushing the heels backward so that the weight of the shoulders falls behind the buttocks, in a vertical line with the heels.

In short, at the sitting trot you push the shoulders and the heels back, and the waist and hands forward.

At first the rider will feel a bit uneasy about withdrawing his shoulders, because he'll do it in the wrong

Fig. 60. Sitting trot with one hand on the quarters.

way. On horseback as on foot, balance can only be preserved, when the shoulders are withdrawn, by curving the loins. Thus it is not "body back" that must be required; it is "**shoulders** back." The pelvis should remain straight and balanced on the seatbones. It is the vertebrae above the pelvis which must move.

The instructor can demonstrate on foot that if he leans his body backward with the small of the back remaining straight, he quickly loses his balance. If he rounds the back, he loses it even more quickly (fig. 61). When the rider does these things on horseback, he thinks his shoulders are back because he can feel himself losing his balance to the rear; but the actual fact is that his shoulders are not back at all, and hence the small of the back hasn't the slightest freedom of movement (fig. 62). Quite the contrary;

Fig. 61. *Bringing the body back with the loins straight or curved out makes you lose your balance.*

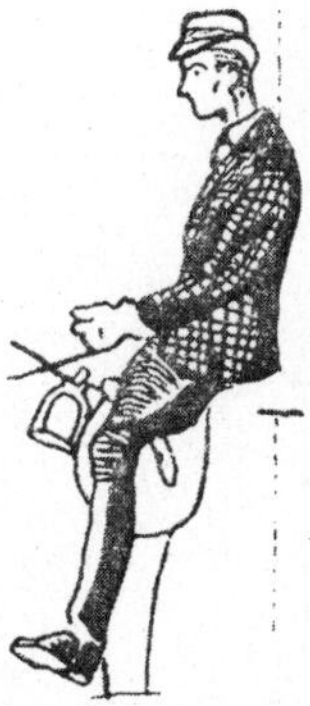

Fig. 62. *This rider thinks he has his shoulders back.*

for on horseback as on foot, only by arching the back can you hold your shoulders back and still maintain your balance (fig. 63).

The thing which prevents riders from drawing their shoulders back sufficiently and in the proper way when they extend their back is a lack of play and suppleness in their loins.

When the rider is doing the sitting trot with his shoulders correctly placed and one hand on the croup, ask him to take up the reins in both hands, while keeping the shoulders just as they were when he had his hand on the croup (fig. 64).

Fig. 63. By arching the loins, one can draw the shoulders back while maintaining balance.

Make sure that the knees do not rise when the rider draws his shoulders back.

Continue the work without stirrups during short but frequent periods of trotting, alternated with rest periods and with exercises involving contact with the horse's mouth.

ଚ୬

The last fifteen minutes of the lesson should be devoted to the control of the horse.

Controlling a horse consists of:
—**initiating the movement;**
—regulating **the movement** (tempo, speed);
—directing **the movement** (direction).

All riding thus depends on forward movement. It

Fig. 64. Sitting trot, with the trunk correctly placed, and the shoulders back.

is just the same with any vehicle, boat, car, or bicycle.

The movement is **regulated** by the legs and hands.

The legs push forward.

The hands, acting to regulate the movement, restrain, stop, or cause to back.

The hands act by tightening the reins. This should be achieved by closing the fingers, with the hands remaining in place or rising if necessary. Do not increase the tension on the reins by withdrawing the elbows toward the rear. ("This; never that!") If the horse does not obey, shorten the reins and repeat the action.

Work hard to develop this good reflex in your pupils.

It is important for the rider to **first** establish constant, soft, elastic contact with the horse's mouth before attempting to control the horse.

The hand must never need to "come back to the horse" before acting to control it.

The rider who acts with reins that are too long, without having first adjusted them, is forced to draw back his elbows and hands in order to establish contact; once they have started back, whether it's accidental or habitual, it is very difficult to stop them at the right place and the right moment, which is to say, as soon as contact has been established.

It is obvious that the legs and hands, since they produce contrary actions, should not act at the same time in regulating movement; this would amount to telling the horse: "Forward, halt!" The rider should be very careful not to let his hands contradict the forward movement or extension of the neck which he has demanded with his legs.[2]

࿊

It is no more necessary to pull on the reins to direct the movement than it is to regulate it.

Be content to have the hands give **instructions** which are addressed to the horse's intelligence, comprehension, and willingness.

In order to communicate these instructions to the horse, it is important first of all to establish contact between the horse's mouth and the rider's hands by adjusting the reins. It is obvious that any attempt to

---

[2] Short movements of the hands toward the horse's poll, a sort of "throwing" the hands forward, give mobility to the head and neck, and elicit or accentuate the play and extension of the head and neck of a horse that tends to stiffen them. These particular hand actions should be coordinated with leg actions that push the horse forward.

communicate through loose reins would be ineffective.

If the horse does not respond to these instructions, **do not reinforce the hand action by pulling on the rein,** but resist with the fingers. **One can only fight resistance in the horse with resistance.** By pulling on the reins, you merely provoke resistance.

If the horse does not obey the resistance of the fingers, don't come back to the horse, but send him with your legs up to the hand. **The horse should feel the bit more strongly only because the legs push him onto it more forcefully. It is the legs which must compel, when necessary, obedience to the hand.**

The hands give direction to the action of the reins; they turn the steering wheel, so to speak, while the legs push the horse into the hands whenever it is necessary to compel obedience or to obtain more prompt, more complete, more perfect obedience.

Never try to coerce a horse with your hands. **It is always abuse from the hand that provokes resistance or defense from the horse.**

This is the concept of riding you must acquire if you wish to have horses that are responsive and easy to control.

༄

*When the rider moves his right hand to the right, the horse **that obeys** moves its head and bends its neck to the right. When the rider pushes forward with both legs, if necessary, the horse turns to the right. **This is the opening rein.***

*The right hand should move frankly to the right, the wrist remaining in the same plane as the forearm, the hand kept at exactly the same height with the **fingernails turning upwards** (fig. 65).*

Turning the nails (or palm) upwards makes the elbows return to the side and prevents them from drawing back, which is an indispensable precondition to producing clear and effective resistance. The rider can thus support the elbows against his side, or at least support the muscles at the back of the arm, if he contracts them; when you need to resist, do so immediately with a well-supported, determined action. Carrying the elbows away from the body by turning the fingernails down will always lead to pulling.

In short, if the rider holds his fingernails up, it is he who is able to resist; if he turns them down, it is the horse that will do so.

If the horse doesn't turn to the right at the indication of the right opening rein, it would be just as

Fig. 65. Opening rein.   *Fig. 66. Supporting rein.*

stupid to try to make it turn right by pulling on the right rein as it would be to pull the tiller of a becalmed boat in order to make it turn. But in both cases, if you push the horse or the boat forward, they will turn.

ಶಿ

*When the rider moves the right hand forward and to the left while pressing the right rein against the **base** of the horse's neck, the horse's head can bend to the right, but, since the neck is being pushed to the left, the horse will turn to the left. **This is the indirect or supporting rein** (fig. 66).*

In order to make the pressure at the base of the neck more effective, the fingernails must be placed up. Demonstrate this to the rider by having him apply a supporting rein, first with his fingernails turned down, and then with the nails up (fig. 67).

The indirect rein has a compelling effect on the

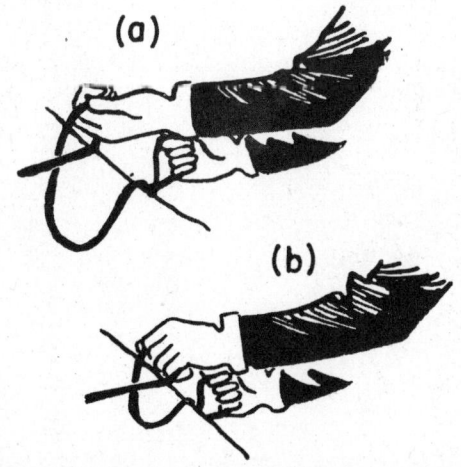

Fig. 67. Supporting rein (a. Ineffective) (b. Effective)

*horse that the opening rein does not possess, for in acting on the base of the neck which is connected to the haunches by muscle,[3] it acts indirectly on **"the haunches, which alone govern the direction"** (General L'Hotte).*

When one hand acts as an opening rein or a supporting rein, **the other hand, after having softly yielded, should maintain its contact, and support the action.**

❧

Since all of this is contrary to our natural reflexes, it is important for the rider to think about what he's doing in order to acquire sound reflexes.

Have the pupil perform a few "doublers"[4] with an opening rein and with a supporting rein, reminding him to **keep his trunk erect,** *which he hardly is likely to do on his own.*

❧

Conclude the lesson with a few minutes of posting trot, ankles, knees, and elbows supple, the line of vision parallel to the ground, and the rider stretching forward into the movement, trotting with the horse.

Relax without stirrups with the trunk erect, reins held at the buckle, and then vault to the ground.

In order **to dismount by vaulting,** you drop your stirrups, take both reins in your left hand and place

---

[3] Ilio-spinal muscle (See *Equitation Raisonnée*).

[4] The "doubler" is a school figure in which the horse leaves the track and moves straight across the ring to the opposite side, where he retakes the track on the same hand. If you wish the rider to change hands after the doubler, the command is: "Doubler and change hands." The rider who was on the right hand, for example, would then make his doubler and turn to the left when he reached the opposite track.

it on top of the horse's neck, and put your right hand on the pommel. Raise yourself on your wrists and swing your right leg over the quarters (fig. 68). Remain poised on your hands for an instant and then

Fig. 68. Vaulting to the ground.

slide lightly to the ground, with heels together and knees flexed.

It is also possible to vault down by dropping the reins entirely and swinging the right leg forward and up over the horse's neck. (Don't be timid about raising the right leg . . .)

CHAPTER V

Fourth Lesson

SUMMARY: Perfecting the posting trot and adherence at the sitting trot without stirrups. Finding the balance of the upper body, and suppling exercises at the sitting trot while checking the erectness of the trunk. The control of the horse: Moving in different directions; an erect upper body is as necessary to the horse as it is for the rider. The extension of the horse's neck promotes obedience. Principles governing resistance. Action of the rein of opposition. Mechanics of the opening rein.

In order to clarify our presentation, from this chapter on we will divide the lessons into two parts: the first will concern the seat; the second, the control of the horse.

This distinction should not be applied literally in actual teaching. The instructor can, and in fact should plan each lesson as he sees fit, alternating work on the seat with work on control, applying the principles of control that have been described in the preceding lessons first to the walk and then to the trot, either on command or as the rider wishes. (The latter is preferable at the beginning, because then the rider will not perform a movement until he is ready, and has thought about it.)

֍

Mount by vaulting. Suppling exercises without stirrups.

Work on the posting trot, constantly seeking the

play of the ankles, keeping the eyes parallel to the ground, the trunk expanded, and minimizing support on the stirrups as much as possible.

Then, the posting trot without stirrups, raising the toes; this is an excellent exercise for developing the support of the rider's calves against the curve of the horse's side as well as for flexing the legs.

Work on the rider's adherence at the sitting trot and the erectness of his trunk by having him place one hand on the horse's croup, with the stomach held forward and the small of the back liberated from the weight of the shoulders.

Employ suppling exercises at the sitting trot, trying to stretch the rider, to get him to engage his pelvis, to seek the "deepest part of the saddle," to hold his shoulders in position, and to expand his upper body. The rider will thereby not only improve his silhouette, but also (especially) his balance. Rotation of the arms, patting the quarters, looking backwards over the shoulder while stretching the upper body, etc.

Though the rider was told during his first lessons at the sitting trot to hold onto the pommel, he should not make a habit of it. He should resort to this means of support as seldom as possible, and only in order to avoid falling. If the rider wishes to progress, he must convince himself that once he's gotten started, holding the pommel is a waste of time.

ప

The rider will not really have a seat until he can do without support from his stirrups and hands. To make yourself stay on solely through the erectness and balance of the trunk, lighten the thighs and stirrups at all the gaits by imperceptibly raising the thighs and by frequently dropping the reins, to prove that you can stay on without any help from them.

These exercises in lightening the thighs, while keeping the heels in position, are very valuable.

Many riders weigh too heavily on their thighs, to the detriment of the pressure of the buttocks in the saddle and thus of the entire seat. You should weight the buttocks, and as heavily as possible; but not the thighs. Lightening the thighs and thus weighting the seat gives greater freedom to the aids (and above all to the legs) for controlling the horse.

Develop in the rider the habit of changing direction while maintaining contact and keeping the wrists well separated, so the new direction is "framed." In riding as in life, one must first know where he wishes to go and then try to move straight toward the chosen goal. This gives us the best chance of getting there. If the rider goes forward without any sense of direction, the horse will wander or go where it pleases. But if the rider fixes his eyes on a definite point, he will communicate his sense of direction to the horse, and it, too, will be drawn in the desired direction. Before turning, select a new destination and make the horse head squarely towards it, while acting with the aids to indicate, and if necessary to push towards, the new direction.

Fight the common beginners' fault of leaning forward when you want to make the horse do something.

By leaning forward, the rider places himself at the horse's mercy; he surrenders to it, he cannot make it surrender to him. He submits to the horse's movements, he cannot command them. In order to make the horse submit, the rider must try to make himself independent of the horse. Only an erect trunk enables the rider to compel the horse to obey. For when the trunk is erect, the rider can momentarily stiffen it at will, permitting him to destroy the horse's resistance by opposing resistance with resistance, and thus forcing the horse to yield. The horse will quickly recognize the stiffening that signifies insurmountable resistance.

An erect trunk also constitutes a safety reflex for the rider. This posture permits him to protect himself both from the action of the horse's neck and mass, and from the force of inertia (which on horseback always tends to throw the rider forward).

By leaning forward, the rider aggravates the problem his own weight poses on the horse's equilibrium. Two-thirds of the weight of a rider who is seated normally is already carried by the forehand.[1]

By leaning forward, the rider overburdens the horse's shoulders and deprives it of both freedom of equilibrium and freedom of movement; the rider puts the horse "on its forehand," making it lean on the hands and hindering its obedience by depriving it of lightness and freedom of movement.

By tipping forward the rider also deprives himself of the freedom and command over his aids that he needs for control. If the actions of the rider's hands and legs are to be effective, they must be supported by the firm base of the pelvis which an erect trunk provides.

The firm base of the pelvis, being located between the legs and the hands, also enables the aids to operate independently of each other, which is essential for easy control of the horse.

The erectness of the upper body is thus just as

---

[1] The horse's body is divided into three parts: the *forehand* (head and neck, shoulders, and forelegs); the *body;* and the *hindquarters* (croup and hindlegs).

necessary for the horse as it is for the rider, since both must preserve their freedom of movement—the horse in order to move easily, and the rider in order to control the horse easily.

*Horse and rider must **both carry themselves independently** and in equilibrium. Only under these circumstances can the rider always be the master of an obedient mount, and regulate and direct its movements instead of submitting to them.*

The seat and the freedom of the aids depend on the amount of weight in the buttocks. The more the rider can weight his buttocks, the better he can use his legs, the better will be his hands, the greater his mastery of the aids. Weighting the buttocks encourages him to resist, rather than pull, with the hands. Weight in the stirrups or thighs, being produced at the expense of weight in the buttocks, both stiffens the legs and encourages pulling on the reins. Bending the legs and keeping the knees supple, however, keeps the heels free. Accordingly, the stirrups should only carry the weight of the legs. It is the same with a man; when he is standing, his weight is in his heels and he is not free to move them, but when he puts his weight in his buttocks by sitting, he can.

Whether the rider uses an opening rein or an indirect rein, any pulling by the hands interferes with the horse's movements and impairs its obedience. Pulling causes either a slackening of gait or a halt by immobilizing the horse's head and neck, or it produces resistance or disobedience, depending on the force of the pull.

When we turn to the right by means of the opening rein, for example, the extension of the horse's head and neck to this side facilitates the movement. In order to make it easy for the horse to be obedient, we must avoid hindering this extension and must, on the contrary, encourage it by advancing the hands, "giving the horse its head," pushing it forward into hands that yield and arms that extend, advancing the hands forward as if pushing a wheelbarrow, and not drawing them back towards the body.

Practice "doublers," telling the rider to advance his hand as if he wished to point out a new direction.

For a horse to be responsive, it must stay "on the aids," that is to say, "before the legs" and "on the bit." If the hand is too harsh it will make the horse drop off the bit and gradually retreat "behind the leg." The horse is then no longer "on the aids," and it can no longer be responsive. This is why one must never "come back to the horse," but rather "send the horse up to the bit." When the horse tries to evade the aids, only the leg can put him back "on the aids," **before the legs and on the bit."**

If the horse resists the instructions of the hands, don't pull, but meet resistance with resistance.

Two essential principles govern opposition to the horse's resistance:

—the fingers should equal the resistance of the horse, and never exceed it (*Lancosme-Brêve*);

—yield as soon as the horse yields.

The rider must thus be alert to the first signs of obedience so that he can diminish the force of his command as soon as the horse **starts** *to obey.*

ಕ∾

When dealing with the right opening rein or the right supporting rein, the left rein still has great importance; for it is the left rein which, by tightening after having yielded in order to let the bit slide over in the horse's mouth, **reinforces the effect of the** *active rein, specifies its direction, and maintains the contact, preserving the horse's forward movement. The horse should be kept in the "corridor" formed by the taut reins. Without contact which encourages the horse to give itself confidently to the rider, the aids cannot control the horse with full effectiveness. **It is the legs,** pushing into the elastic support of the rider's elbows, which oblige the horse to stretch into the forward movement.*

Most of the problems encountered in riding originate nowhere else than in improper use of the aids. It is worth repeating that riders are tempted too often to blame the horse.

*For example, when turning to the right with an opening rein, as soon as the right hand has indicated the direction of movement with the right rein, and resisted if necessary, and as soon as the left hand has supported, **the hands have done their job.** Doing anything more would only hinder the horse's obedience, and provoke or increase resistance.*

*When the rider encounters resistance in the horse, **the remedy is not in the hands, but in the legs.** There is really only one remedy: **ride forward!***

This is particularly evident when using the opening rein, which is the normal "steering" rein.

*Let's assume that the rider wishes to make a right turn with an opening rein. He moves the right hand to the right. Naturally, the horse responds to this rein action by trying to move its nose **to the left** (action = reaction). The rider resists by closing the fingers of the right hand. The horse, feeling this resistance, yields in order to stop the pressure of the ring of the bit against the left side of its mouth; it moves its head to the right, and bends its neck to the right, **but this alone does not oblige it to turn to the right.** If it does* *not turn, what does the rider (not only beginners, either) do? He pulls on the right rein, imagining that he will force the horse to turn to the right. Now the horse bends its entire spine to the right; in doing so, the right hindleg is engaged further underneath its body than the left one; and, since the horse moves like an ice-skater (the right hindleg pushing the horse forward and toward the left, the left hindleg pushing it forward and toward the right) the horse has been perfectly prepared by the rider to push itself **toward the left** (fig. 69). And the more the rider pulls on the right rein, the more the horse will push itself to the left! This horse isn't being disobedient—it is obeying scrupulously. And this is one more proof that there*

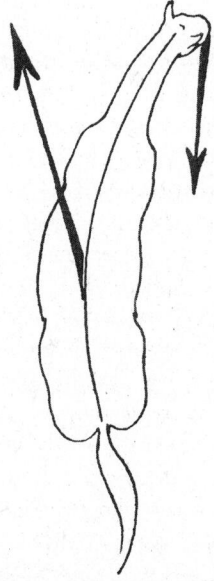

Fig. 69. Pulling the right rein helps the horse to push left.

are no disobedient horses, there are only riders who are clumsy or inept.

The error in this case was pulling on the right rein. The remedy would be: **pushing** *with both legs into the resisting fingers of the right hand, i.e., going forward! Then, tightening the left rein to make a barrier on the left and prevent the horse from escaping to that side.*

Deductions: *The shoulders are always governed by the haunches, and not the opposite.*

The head and neck have no more compelling effect on the horse's direction than a tiller has upon a boat that is standing still, or being swept along by a current that is stronger than its own propulsion. In both cases, the remedy lies neither in the neck nor in the helm, but rather in increasing the propulsion. This is the decisive factor which makes the action of the helm or of the rider's hands effective, and obtains yielding and obedience.

The hands are always used too much in riding, and the legs not enough.

Never persist in using methods which do not produce immediate obedience. If the horse does not obey, it is because the rider is not doing the right thing. Accordingly, try something else. And, since man's natural reflexes on horseback are always wrong, it is not stupid at all to say that if you have not obtained obedience in one way, you should often do just the opposite.

ථ

To help the rider develop the habit of using the opening rein correctly, tell him, for example: "When I tell you to, you will doubler to the right. Be sure your trunk is correctly balanced on your seatbones.

Adjust your reins and your legs. Using an opening rein, doubler." If the horse does not obey immediately: *"Tighten your calves. Ride forward. Push!"* If the horse drifts to the left: *"Resist with the left rein. Don't pull, push!"* Repeat these things endlessly, so that they really sink into the pupils' heads and develop the correct reflexes: *"Don't pull, push! Don't come back to the horse! Push it up to your hands!"*

"Don't pull. Push."

In order not to pull, the trunk must be erect, and the fingernails turned up (*so that the resistance is supported*).

In order to push, *you must weight the buttocks, keep the legs flexed and the knees supple (to free the heels), and the heels down (to harden the calves).*

Apply these principles while doing doublers at a walk, and then at a sitting trot with stirrups.

CHAPTER VI

Fifth Lesson

SUMMARY: Developing the play of the loins at the sitting trot. Control: Causes of the principal difficulties encountered by beginners. "The haunches alone govern direction." Using the upper body as an aid. Coordinating the action of the body with the outside lateral aids. Strike-offs into the canter.

Most riders can follow the progression outlined in these lessons, but those who cannot keep up will have to repeat lessons. It is better to build only on solid ground. The method must be adapted to the pupil, and not the reverse.

In the interest of clarity, however, we will continue our presentation in the form of lessons. Moreover, it has been our experience that the vast majority of students can follow the lessons as they are outlined in this book.

ஓ

Begin the lesson, as usual, with suppling exercises and improving the posting trot. Work on the erectness and balance of the trunk at the sitting trot. Perform corrective suppling exercises.

ஓ

By now, the rider's trunk should be well placed at the sitting trot. The small of the back, freed from the weight of the shoulders and limbered by suppling exercises in extension and rotations, is able to play freely. The instructor can now try to develop a cadenced action of the rider's back at the sitting trot, which will facilitate the balance of the body and develop coordination.

One cannot preserve one's balance on a moving object except by moving too, not by seeking a fixed position. The more the rider stiffens himself, the more he feels the concussion. **The only way to accompany a movement is to make movements that match those which you wish to minimize.**

The vertical jolting at the trot results from the horse's regular up and down movements. In order to absorb the shock of the rising movements, the rider's back and loins must flex (fig. 70). After having risen, the horse's body descends faster than the rider's. In order to be able to follow the horse's descending movement promptly, the rider must, on the one hand, have his calves engaged against the horse's body; and on the other, simultaneously extend his back and loins. This extension, combined with the support of the calves from front to back, shifts the pelvis and the knees forward and downward (counter-actions), presses the buttocks and thighs to the saddle, and ensures the preservation of adherence (fig. 71). The rider who doesn't function this way, whose back does not extend freely, will hit the saddle during the following rising movement; the result is a succession of "paddle strokes" which bounce him out of the saddle at each hoofbeat. Thus it is the horse that makes the rider's back flex, but it is the rider who must initiate the ensuing extending movement. The flexing movements are produced passively, **the extending movements must, at the beginning, be made actively.**

It is not possible to move the trunk supply and easily enough, and also maintain equilibrium, unless

Fig. 70. Flexing the loins absorbs the rising movement.

Fig. 71. Extending the back and loins permits adherence to be preserved.

the back can play alternately in **flexion and in extension.** This is equally true on foot and on horseback.

The instructor can demonstrate this on foot. While walking slowly, as he puts his foot down he extends the small of the back, then as the other foot moves forward he flexes it, and so forth (fig. 72).

Fig. 72. Moving the upper body on foot while preserving balance.

By proceeding in the same way on horseback, you can easily flex and extend your trunk and still maintain equilibrium, just as on foot.

To give the pupil the trotting rhythm, have him sit to the trot and make short hand movements toward the horse's mouth, in cadence with the beats of the trot, while the instructor calls the tempo of these movements, "tick-tock, tick-tock." The movement of the rider's elbows as they graze past his waist will gradually bring about rhythmic extensions of his back.

While this exercise is being performed the rider

should constantly try to maintain his balance on the seatbones, lowering his knees, and pushing the shoulders and heels backward, and the waist and hands forward in cadence with the trot. **Stretch** and **expand** the front of the body; throw out the chest, while rhythmically stretching the upper body in cadence with the trot.

This exercise will develop the flexibility and coordination which the rider lacks, and will help to break the habit of hanging on with the hands.

ಶ್

Most riding difficulties encountered by beginners are caused by:
*—**reins that are too long**,*
*—actions that are **too late**;*
*—actions that are **too prolonged**.*

ಶ್

***Reins too long:** Faulty rein adjustment results in faulty support, unsteady contact with the horse's mouth, and thus, insufficient impulsion in the horse. The horse does not feel, or does not feel clearly enough, actions of the reins which under these conditions are confused and lack clarity and authority.*

***Actions too late:** The beginner waits until the horse's disobedience has actually occurred before taking action. He must acquire faster reflexes. By precise, authoritative actions of the supporting reins, he should immediately correct a horse that is starting to deviate from the desired direction. Before the horse actually leaves the line of direction or the track, the rider should feel that it is leaning away from it; **this is the moment**, immediately and without hesitation, when the hands must move decisively to restore the* *horse to the track, while the legs increase the forward movement, if this is necessary in order to reinforce the hand action, and increase the horse's obedience if needed.*

ಜೀ

Actions too prolonged: We must always bear in mind the horse's momentum and the way its head and neck swing. If the rider continues his hand actions until the horse's head and neck actually reach the desired direction, the horse will go past it. Thus it is important for the rider to guard against prolonging his hand actions any more than is necessary. Yield earlier, and substitute a series of shorter actions, until the horse is placed in the desired direction.

When the rider's actions are late or too prolonged, the horse cannot stay straight, but will move in a serpentine.

Apply these principles by having the rider frequently change from one direction to another, at the walk and sitting trot.

Since problems of control are even more persistent for the beginner than problems of the seat, don't hesitate to clarify the underlying principles thoroughly, and to find different ways of explaining them, all leading to the same conclusion: "Don't pull. Push." Push the resistance, if the horse resists, but push into hands that yield and arms that advance as soon as the horse yields.

"The haunches alone govern directons" (General L'Hotte). The horse's shoulders are governed by the haunches, not the reverse. It is the horse's right hindleg that pushes it to the left, and the left hindleg that pushes to the right (and the same is true of us). Consequently, bring the horse's shoulders over (opening

rein) or push them (indirect rein) in the direction of the turn, but don't hinder their forward movement. The shoulders could not, in effect, gain their place in the new direction from the propulsion of the hindlegs, for these push laterally only during forward movement. Most of the resistance encountered in turning thus originates either in hands which prevent the horse's shoulders from moving forward, or from insufficient impulsion. If the rider prevents the shoulders from moving forward, they move out, and tend to escape to the opposite side from the one toward which the rider wishes to go.

To help the rider develop authority in his turning controls, tell him to brace himself on his inside seatbone (making it easy to momentarily stiffen the spine, during the fingers' very brief moment of resistance, if the horse does not immediately respond to the hand) and to face squarely the new direction while stretching the upper body.

As the rider begins to understand the mechanics of the aids, make him feel how he can further diminish his hand actions in turning by using his upper body as an aid. Weight the right seatbone in order to turn to the right, and the left seatbone in order to turn to the left, without moving the loins sideways, but with the trunk held as a single unit. The rider's body weight thus influences the horse's equilibrium. His upper body induces, instead of being carried along (fig. 73).

Have the rider feel how powerful the supporting rein becomes when combined with this weight aid. The upper body encourages, "come this way" in the same direction indicated by the supporting rein's push, "go there!" To turn to the right, for example, having checked the erectness of the trunk and in-

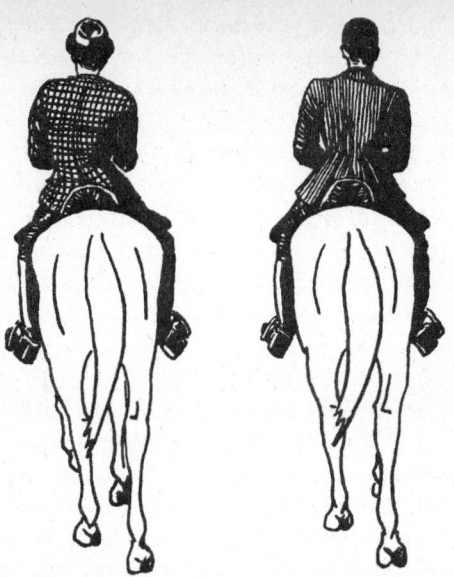

Fig. 73. Use of the upper body as an aid.

creased the weight on the buttocks by increasing the suppleness of the knees, the rider weights his right seatbone, while his left hand, **nails up,** pushes the base of the horse's neck forward and to the right, the right hand acting only as if to point a finger at the new direction, but without losing contact entirely.

The action of the outside lateral aids reinforces the horse's natural movements, and thus has a powerful effect on the horse; hence the left supporting rein and left leg are used for turning to the right, and inversely.

Have the rider do doublers this way at a walk, and serpentines at the sitting trot.

Another pedestrian's reflex which must be destroyed (and which is certainly not only a beginner's *reflex): lowering the hand on the side of the turn, which causes pulling and robs the hand of precision and clarity. With an obedient horse, the hands should remain at the same height when indicating turns (opening or indirect rein). But if the horse is difficult to turn to the right, for example, it is better to raise the right hand slightly and to lower the left hand, which is just the opposite of what many riders do. (It's also opposite to the way we use the steering wheel of a car).*

In order to obtain the maximum effect from the upper body you must straighten it; leaning forward reduces the influence of this aid.

Bracing yourself on the seatbone on the side of the turn tends to support the hands so that they weigh less heavily on the horse's mouth.

Facing squarely towards the new direction automatically helps to produce appropriate actions of the aids.

ಕ✒

Toward the end of this lesson, the rider can be safely permitted to canter, first with stirrups, and then without.

To strike off into a canter you push into yielding hands and arms that advance.

Remind the rider that you can only maintain balance on a moving object by making **movements that synchronize** with the movement of the object. The more the rider stiffens, the more he will feel the concussion. Ask the rider to move his upper body just as he did at the sitting trot, but in cadence with the canter's slightly slower tempo. Accompany the movements of the canter by trying to stay on entirely by means of the erectness and balance of the upper body.

Especially at the canter, bend the knees, and keep them supple, for pressing on the stirrups would weaken the seat; and don't hang on with the reins. "You never fall off backwards, you always fall off forwards. Take your choice."

༄

Cantering can be begun even more safely by mounting the pupil on a horse on the longe and using a "voltige surcingle" (which has hand grips)—but this isn't really necessary at all. The rider who has been trained from the beginning with our methods can go right into the canter without worrying about falling off. He has learned how to stick on by engaging his calves when he needs to. The means of staying on which have been taught him, and which he has already proven to himself, are quite sufficient.

CHAPTER VII

Sixth and Seventh Lessons

SUMMARY: Perfecting the seat at the sitting trot by moving with the horse. Sitting trot with the toes hanging naturally. Suppling exercises at the sitting trot. The seat at the canter. "To go to the right, prevent the horse from going to the left." Elastic compression. Control through intermittent actions of the aids.

Improve the seat at the sitting trot without stirrups by trying to get the rider to move *with* the horse.

From now on, the rider will benefit from performing the sitting trot with his toes hanging naturally. He should raise them intentionally only if he needs a stronger grip in an emergency.

To develop the balancing ability of the upper body which the rider needs, have him do suppling exercises at the sitting trot which put him in awkward situations, and thus upset his balance, making him compensate instinctively. (Torsions of the loins, looking backwards or patting the quarters, turning around in the saddle, holding one arm horizontally, etc.) Continue to have him **stretch** and **expand** his body in front in order to free the back more and more from the weight of the shoulders, and thus develop its maximum freedom of action.

When the rider is balanced on his seatbones and

moving with the horse, ask him to seek the deepest part of the saddle by bringing the pelvis into play, and have him rhythmically push his hips toward his elbows.

In order to increase the coordination and suppleness of the loins, have him trot, pushing the knees down and the heels back at each beat of the trot, at each extending movement of the back.

ಒ

In the canter, the rider is subjected to the horizontal jolting that arises from variations of speed at this gait. The flexing of the back and loins which preceeds the relaxation of the hindlegs should immediately be followed by the inverse movement during the rising of the quarters (conserving the rider's adherence to the saddle) (fig. 74).

The alternating play of the back and loins between flexion and extension creates an undulating movement which carries from vertebra to vertebra along the whole length of the rider's spine. When the rider has acquired sufficient suppleness, his head and shoulders show the least displacement; it is at the level of the waist that the swings of the rider's vertebrae attain maximum amplitude. This is the way, with the shoulders moving little and staying in line with the heels, that the rider achieves the best seat.

Make sure that the rider does not allow the flexing movements of the spine to predominate. In order to maintain a judicious balance, the rider's spine (and not merely the small of the back) should oscillate between equal degrees of flexion and extension on either side of the balanced position.

Because the sequence of rocking movements which he must accompany at the canter is rapid, if the rider

Fig. 74. Back and loin movements of the rider at the canter.

permits flexions to predominate or exaggerates them, his spine will not have time to straighten and then to act in extension. The rider who attempts to "crush the small of the back into the saddle," following an old but senseless precept, loses his ease of movement and all possibility of correctly sitting to the canter.

The rider must thus try to keep a certain tension in his back, even restricting the flexing movements a bit if necessary at the beginning, and accentuating if anything the movements of extension, which by nature are not as easy to make as the flexions.

Have your riders canter, not crushed into their saddles, but erect, stretching the body up and pushing the stomach forward in cadence with the gallop. They will improve not only their silhouette, but above all their balance and coordination.

At the canter as at other gaits, the rider will not have a seat **until he can do without the support of the hands and stirrups** (lighten the thighs and stirrups, and frequently slacken the reins).

೭∾

Especially at the canter, both horse and rider must **carry themselves.** Refuse to give the horse the exaggerated support it seeks; drop its head entirely to make it carry its own weight. Pulling on the reins of a horse that leans on them will only make the horse lean more.

೭∾

Many difficulties in control arise because the riders think only about the horse's head. They think, for example, that if they turn its nose to the right, the horse will necessarily turn in that direction.

It is the contrary, however, that is true. A horse whose head and neck are bent to the right (a bending which naturally carries down the back) is best prepared to propel itself to the left (through increased engagement of the right hindleg which pushes its mass to the left). If the horse fails to stretch into the forward movement because of laziness, unwilling-

ness, or the fault of the rider, it will evade the direction of the turn, the base of the neck escaping to the left and carrying the horse that way. The cause of this disobedience is the horse's **lack of forward impulsion** in the direction of the turn, a defect which shows up as **lateral evasion.**

Thus it is not the horse's nose which is especially important in steering—the nose is merely incidental—**it is the base of the horse's neck.** The nose and head can be completely divorced from the rest of the mechanism, like a weathervane. The same is not true of the base of the neck, which is connected by muscles to the haunches, which **alone determine direction.**

Accordingly, it is principally the base of the neck which the rider must think about; this is the part he must place or hold on the curve of the turn.

That is why we say, "If you want to go to the right, prevent the horse from going to the left."

This expression is not a pun, as it might first seem. For it is the actions of the left rein and the left leg, forming a barrier to the left and preventing the horse from deviating to that side, which exert the most decisive effect in the turn to the right and oblige the horse to obey the command of the right hand, whose action is then restricted to a simple indication of direction.

In order to create this barrier to the left, lower the left hand to keep **the base** of the neck in place, and lower the left heel to harden the left calf, as if you wished to prevent the horse's side from sticking out under the heel. The action of the left leg is supported by the right leg and the right seatbone.

The horse can only accept the bit if it trusts the rider's hands; only then can it "yield its head." In order to stretch forward the horse needs elastic sup-

port from the rider's elbows, and reins (constantly and lightly tautened) which enclose the base of the neck.

A horse that fears the rider's hands will invert its neck and put its nose at the height of the ears—an attempt to spare its bars the jerks inflicted by a heavy hand, or the pulling that results from clumsy efforts to hang on or steer—and in this posture it is incapable of preserving forward impulsion.

It is always the legs which create, maintain, or increase the horse's elastic compression. The hands encourage it only by supporting, by making the horse aware of the elasticity of the elbows.

Elastic compression consolidates the horse's nose and upper neck with the base of the neck. It turns the whole neck into one unit. And the more rigid this block becomes **due to the action of the rider's legs,** *the greater effect the hand actions can have on the haunches.*

The horse can be represented by a simple model which the instructor can make and have his pupils handle to their benefit. This model (fig. 75) is composed of three blocks of wood representing the horse's quarters (the largest block), its shoulders, and its head. These three blocks are joined together by a spring.

Everything that we have said about riding can be demonstrated with this gadget:

If you simply pull on the right rein without using any other aid, the shoulder block will escape to the left.

If you pull or push the shoulder block to the right without shifting it backwards the mechanism will turn easily when you push the quarters forward.

Tightening the left rein prevents lateral deviation of the shoulders when you wish to turn to the right.

Fig. 75. Model for demonstrating the action of the rider's aids.

The elasticity of the neck, sustained by contact through the reins, induces an elastic shortening of the back which permits the actions of the hands to affect the haunches.

It should be noted that, because of the horse's muscular interrelationships, the forward and rear springs are in one piece; one of them cannot be compressed without compressing the other, and if one of them is released, the other is too.

But—and this is important—on horseback **it is by means of the rear spring that you must try to compress the front spring,** or to increase its elasticity so that the horse will stretch **into the forward movement** and remain "on the aids," in front of the legs, and on the bit.

Control exercises (turns) at a walk and sitting trot,

making the outside lateral aids predominate, using the trunk and always trying to minimize the role of the hands, employing them to make indications that are more and more limited in intensity and duration. Serpentines, alternately weighting one seatbone and then the other, with **the legs always prepared to push** *at the horse's slightest sluggishness in obeying.*

An excellent procedure for fighting the rider's natural tendency to pull on the rein on the side to which he wishes to turn: to turn to the right, move the right hand forward and push the horse to the right with the left supporting rein; weight the right seatbone, the trunk erect; use the predominant action of the left leg supported by the right seatbone; face squarely the new point of direction. This way the horse will turn "automatically."

ঌ

Perform "voltes" at a walk and at a sitting trot.[1]

In order to control the horse while hindering its movements as little as possible, tell the rider not to keep his hands to the right, for example, for the entire duration of the volte to the right. Transmit commands not by continuing actions which weigh down the horse's mouth, but **by brief and intermittent actions.** *Make the volte through a series of brief actions which alternately yield in response to each yielding of the horse: action, yielding, action, yielding, etc. Move the right hand to the right, then bring it back to position; to the right, to position, etc. This should be practiced with the opening rein as well as with the supporting rein. In the latter case, the rider acts as if he wished to brush the horse's mane at the base*

[1] A "volte" is a circle which starts from and returns to the track.

of its neck the other way by successive actions, their frequency depending on the horse's obedience: Push. The horse yields, yield. Push, etc.

This kind of action lightens the rider's hand, and makes it animated and alive. And all things that are animated and alive are easier to bear than those that are inert and consequently heavier. The rider thus can control his horse while hindering its movements as little as possible.

Now teach the rider to use the same kind of brief, successive actions to bring the horse to a halt: resistance, yielding; resistance, yielding. These actions are made by the little fingers, with the thumbs remaining fixed.

The rider should avoid letting the horse feel the weight of his hands. He should try to make it feel the elasticity of his elbows. **There are no hard mouths, there are only heavy hands.** *If you have a light hand, you will have light horses.* **Horses are capable of obeying indications and commands that are infinitely lighter than is usually thought.**

Reduce the rider's actions to a minimum. Afford the horse the maximum freedom of movement and initiative that is compatible with the rider's needs.

CHAPTER VIII

Eighth Lesson

SUMMARY: Sitting trot and canter. Moving **with** the horse at the canter. Weighting the left side facilitates the strike-off into a canter on the right lead.

Improve the sitting trot (suppling exercises) and the canter.

Ask the rider to press as little as possible on the stirrups; to **lighten the thighs,** with knees supple and legs bent; and to weight the buttocks and seek the deepest part of the saddle, while bringing the pelvis more and more into play, shoulders back, and chest expanded to free the back from the weight of the shoulders.

Especially at the canter, seek to balance the trunk on the seatbones and move **with** the horse.

ತಿ

Help the rider to acquire the feeling of the canter's rhythm by counting (one-two-three; one-two-three).

At the canter as at the walk, the horse moves its head and neck. Thus the rider must not fix his hands, but must follow the horse's neck movements with the play of his elbows, emphasizing, as at the walk, the forward hand movement which accompanies the lowering-extending movement of the horse's neck and head.

When the rider has learned to maintain contact

with the horse's neck movements at the canter he can easily regulate the gait, either extending it (by rhythmically pushing with the legs into arms that stretch forward, thereby accentuating the extending movements of the horse's head and neck) or shortening it (by limiting the horse's extension) or changing the cadence of the canter at will (by regulating the cadence of the neck movements).

It is clear that to be able to keep contact with the neck movements at the canter by means of the play of the elbows, and even more to be able to regulate them, the rider's hands must somehow get support from a firm seat. Remind the rider that he can never have a firm seat unless he can do without the support of the stirrups and reins. This is even more obvious at the canter than at the other gaits.

In order to facilitate the canter on the right lead, for example, as well as the strike-off into this lead, tell the rider to weight his left seatbone.[1]

ঌ

The horse canters **on the right lead** when the right forefoot is placed down ahead of the left forefoot and the right hindfoot leads the left hindfoot (fig. 76).

The horse **canters true** when it is on the right lead when turning to the right or when the rider is on the right hand in the riding ring.

The horse is **on the false lead** when it takes the right lead while turning to the left or when the rider is on the left hand in the riding ring.

[1] In the canter on the right lead, the horse holds itself back with the left hindleg and propels itself forward with the right. Consequently, you must weight the left side when you wish to slow down, and the right side when you wish to extend the stride.

The horse is **disunited** when its forelegs are on the right lead while the hindlegs are on the left, or vice versa (fig. 77).

Fig. 76. Canter on the right lead.

Fig. 77. Disunited canter.

CHAPTER IX

Ninth Lesson

SUMMARY: Sitting trot. Canter without stirrups, the toes raised. Jumping "without reins." Turning at the canter (supporting rein).

Review the basics of the sitting trot letting the toes hang naturally, and of the canter without stirrups with the toes raised.

Try to get the rider to move by keeping his back, elbows and knees supple. At the canter, it is not so much the shoulders that should move, but the small of the back and waist. The pelvis and shoulders obviously cannot remain immobile, but the rider should seek to limit their movements as much as possible, for they occur at the expense of the movement of the small of the back.

Get the rider habitually to follow the horse's neck movements at the canter through the play of his elbows. At the same time, make him expand his trunk (silhouette and balance).

Starting with this lesson, the rider's seat can be improved by having him ride over "cavaletti," the reins held at the buckle, with the feet in the stirrups at first, and then without stirrups, raising the toes.[1]

As soon as the horse is straightened out and squarely presented to the first of the cavaletti, the

[1] "Cavaletti" are rails at a height of 20" to 24", supported by feet at each end (fig. 78).

rider holds the reins in only one hand, at the buckle. In this way he will be forced to jump without hanging onto the reins. **Make sure that the rider does not look down at the obstacle as he jumps,** but continues to gaze far ahead, his chin forward. He encircles the horse with his calves while raising the toes, and lets himself go forward, yielding to the force of inertia as the horse slackens its speed preceding the takeoff. At this moment, the rider must get ahead of his horse in order not to be behind it when landing. During the "bascule" over the obstacle, the rider's back acts in extension, but his shoulders remain forward. At no moment during the jump is it helpful to round the back (fig. 78).

Point out to the rider—and if he gets a chance to feel it for himself, so much the better—that if the horse refuses and he tightens his knees, his odds are good (if that's the word!) of shooting over the horse's neck. But if he keeps his knees supple and presses his calves against the curve of the horse's sides from front to back, he will stay on.

During all of this schooling over fences, make the rider "seek the horse's side behind his boot," girdling the horse with his calves in order to make him feel that it is the support point established by the calves, against the horse's side near the girth, which provides him with the most effective means of staying on.

In order to give the rider good reflexes at the canter, have him advance the hand that is on the side of the turn; for example, when the rider wishes to turn to the right, have him slightly advance his right hand, not to a point that leaves the horse without support, but enough to let the indirect rein predominate.

Fig. 78. *Jumping without reins.*

This procedure effectively combats the rider's natural reflex of always pulling on the right rein when he wishes to turn to the right, which is contrary to the natural movements of the horse.

CHAPTER X

Tenth Lesson

SUMMARY: Rhythmic suppling exercises at the canter. Rhythmic action of the legs and play of the elbows at the canter. The gallop in supple suspension. Jumping series of cavaletti without reins. Striking off into a canter. Halting from a canter. Backing.

Rhythmic suppling exercises at the canter without stirrups, the rider alternately patting the horse's shoulder and flank in cadence with the gallop, counting aloud if necessary, while stretching the upper body from time to time and continuing to envelop the horse with his legs.

In order to develop coordination at the canter and make the rider feel the rhythm of this gait, have him periodically squeeze the horse's sides with his calves, smoothly and softly, in cadence with the canter, his hands placed on the horse's mane and pushing its neck forward at each stride. This exercise can be performed either at a sitting canter, or at a canter in supple suspension (in which the rider stands in his stirrups, just as for the trot in supple suspension which was previously described).

The canter in supple suspension markedly develops the rider's stability and the envelopment by his legs (fig. 79).

ಕಾ

At the end of the lesson, jump two, three, or four successive cavaletti about 20 feet apart "without

Fig. 79. The canter in supple suspension.

reins," raising the toes and above all **not looking at the rails.**

You should never look at the obstacle you are jumping (except from a distance, of course). In this way, no matter where the horse makes its takeoff, the rider is always "with the horse." This is an excellent habit to instill at the beginning, and an excellent procedure to preserve later on when jumping bigger fences. The horse will also extend more fully over the jump if the rider stretches into the forward movement while looking far beyond the obstacle. Moreover, the horse has a better chance of holding a straight line, or of being straightened in time, if the rider picks a point *on the far side of the obstacle with the intention of riding toward it.*

Accustom the rider to "ride" the horse over the obstacle, by having him smoothly and softly squeeze his calves in cadence with the stride at the instructor's rhythmic, "Now! Now! Now!"

In order to vary the rhythm of the jumping efforts (which is very beneficial for the development of the rider's seat) vary the distances between the "cavaletti," placing the two or three first ones, for example, 20 to 25 feet apart, and the two final ones at a distance of 12 or 13 feet.

ಕ⋑

Practice strike-offs into the canter from a sitting trot, with the rider weighting his outside buttock and pushing with both legs while using the hands to burden and retard the outside lateral legs.

In order to strike off into a canter on the right lead, for example, weight the left buttock (knees supple), move both hands forward and toward the left, and push the horse into a canter by means of **energetic action by both legs.**

Most beginners do not use their legs with enough energy and decisiveness to get into the canter. When the leg actions are not sufficiently authoritative, the horse will simply extend the trot more and more. The extended trot is a very taxing gait, which tires horses much more quickly than does the canter.

The rider should therefore use leg actions which are authoritative, energetic, and **decisive** *enough to make the horse move directly from a controlled trot into a canter; sort of "breaking" it into a canter, with-*

out passing through the extended trot which is so tiring.

ཚ༔

Have the rider make some halts from the canter, his fixed hands supported by the firm base of the pelvis, the hips drawn close to the hands [1) with the back, 2) with the hands], the trunk expanded, the chest thrown out.

Teach the rider to back, fingers closed on the reins while raising the hands, using intermittent actions. Be satisfied with just a few backing steps.

ཚ༔

After this lesson, the pupil can go out and ride cross-country without fear.

When riding cross-country, the rider should do as little as possible, letting the horse move in supervised freedom, so to speak, while he relies on the horse's instinct and affords it all the initiative and liberty he can, consistent with control. ***Use the hands as little as possible if you want the horse to be as agreeable as possible.***

ཚ༔

Now the rider can only wait for time and practice to develop his adaptation and his reflexes.

But he must work while waiting. The fact that he has completed these ten lessons does not mean that he can consider himself fully trained. He should return from time to time to the watchful eye of the riding instructor, who will correct the bad habits that have developed when working outdoors and alone, and who will hunt out the bad natural instincts which always tend, as the saying goes, "to come back at a gallop."

It will be very worthwhile for the rider who is working alone to review these lessons **many** times in order to be sure that he is staying on the right track.

Though lessons can certainly shorten the training period, even the best of them cannot replace the time and practice that are necessary for the rider's adaptation and the firm establishment of correct reflexes.

CHAPTER XI

The Gaits

The **walk** is a gait in which the horse's feet strike the ground one after the other. If the horse starts to walk from a halt, and its right forefoot initiates the gait, the other feet are placed in the following order: left hind, left fore, right hind (fig. 80).

The horse walks at a speed of about 4 miles an hour, and covers a mile in fifteen minutes.

The walk is the gait which the horse can maintain for the longest time without tiring. It is better, however, to break very long walks with short periods of trotting.

Since the horse uses its head and neck as a counterweight at the walk, the rider should not deprive it of the freedom of movement of its head and neck, at the risk of causing an unnecessary waste of energy.

≥∞

The **trot** is a gait at which the horse places each diagonal pair of legs successively on the ground[1] (fig. 81).

The horse trots at about 9 miles an hour, and covers a mile in seven minutes.

An even trot, alternated with periods of walking

[1] The right diagonal consists of the right foreleg and the left hindleg; the left diagonal, of the left foreleg and the right hindleg.

Fig. 80. The walk.

Fig. 81. The trot.

depending on the horse's condition, is the most suitable gait for covering long distances.

At the trot the horse immobilizes its head and neck. At the ordinary trot, this tautness of the horse's neck facilitates its propulsion (supporting the elbows).

ৡ

The **canter** is a rocking gait. At the canter on the right lead, the horse places the left hindleg, the left diagonal, and the right fore, and marks a period of suspension before placing the left hindleg again (fig. 82).

At the canter, the horse moves at a speed of about 12 miles an hour, and covers a mile in about five minutes. At the gallop, the speed is 15 to 20 miles per hour, and a mile is covered in three to four minutes, or even less.

The rider should not gallop for long stretches.

ৡ

At all gaits, it is important to permit the horse's head and neck to extend, giving him the maximum freedom of movement of this counter-balance (and thus using his strength and agility most economically).

It is better to go into the canter than to extend the trot. The extended trot is the most tiring gait of all for a horse.

Because of the instability of the horse's equilibrium as well as the muscular effort required at the canter and gallop, the horse's head and neck movements are particularly important at these gaits.

Since the horse possesses the same physiological pattern as a man, the same rules should be applied to its work. A well-planned daily program consists of:

Fig. 82. The canter.

warming-up, the actual workout, and the cooling-off.

When the horse begins to sweat, it is the rider who has done too much.

CHAPTER XII

"Rational Jumping"

"The rational seat," acquired by the method that has just been presented, leads perfectly naturally to "rational jumping," which has now been adopted by riders of all countries.

Rational jumping is characterized by the engagement of the calves under the diameter of the horse's body, by the backward pressure of the calves against the curvature of the horse's side, and by the rider's being in balance before, during and after the jump. The horse's jump acts upon the angles formed by the rider's joints, and the rider holds himself in supple suspension when the horse returns to earth during the landing stride after the jump. This supple suspension, which the rider achieves through elastic play of the ankles, knees and hips, makes him lighter, facilitates the play of the horse's back and loin, and permits the maximum utilization of its capacities, and thus the maximum end-result[1] (fig. 83).

Training for the rational jump is based first on exercises at a trot and canter in supple suspension. Then, when the rider can easily remain balanced on his calves without reins, he should jump in supple suspension and without reins over cavaletti placed at different distances; and finally, he should jump successively higher fences under the same conditions.

---

[1] See *Equitation Raisonnée* by the same author.

Fig. 83. Jumping larger fences.

CHAPTER XIII

Further Improvement

When the rider has acquired an adequate seat—and this requires a great deal of practice—he can progress to intermediate and then to advanced equitation, and, if he is talented, after much time and work, to Haute Ecole, a sphere in which very few riders can ever move with assurance.

Once the rider has developed an absolutely unshakeable seat, which provides him with perfect control over his aids, he can seek further to develop the quality of his hands.

The hands, having become perfectly attentive, will thus begin to perceive the slightest yielding of the horse's neck or jaw. The rider will establish communication with the horse by answering resistance with resistance, and by responding instantly to its yielding with a yielding of the elbows or fingers, to its lightness with more lightness, to elasticity with greater elasticity. He will thus succeed in creating a relationship that is more and more supple and elastic, and more and more perfect.

After thus developing the tact of the hand, the rider can learn truly to use his legs.

For when he has acquired hands of sufficient quality, he can become more exacting with his legs.

He will reach the point where his legs command

the lateral bending and the flexing movements of the horse's back, which is the origin of all the movements controlled by the rider's legs; the haunches, source of the horse's motive power; and the movements of its limbs.

As the rider progresses, his legs substitute more and more for the hands in controlling the horse. They too must acquire the tact and precision that are essential to being able to act at exactly the right moment for the movement which the rider wishes to obtain.[1]

Fig. 84. The horse "gathered."

By means of the spur, the rider can develop the sensitivity of his legs until they equal the quality of

[1] See *Equitation Raisonnée* by the same author.

his hands, producing a horse that is just as responsive to the legs as it is to the hand.

He will then have become a real horseman.

As you see, it is not only "good hands" that make a rider, as many people believe. Good hands are only one step on the long road the rider must travel before he deserves to be called "a good rider." **It is the legs that make the rider.**

A fine rider is no longer satisfied merely to pro-

Fig. 85. Collection.

duce, maintain, or accelerate **movement** with his legs; he uses them to generate the impulsion that the hands then utilize to direct, to gather, to slow down, to back, to support, to maneuver the horse in all directions, to regulate the movements of its legs and the different gaits.

૨☙

Through the elastic support of the horse's forehand, and the engagement of its haunches, the rider will produce the "gathering" (*ramener*) in which the horse becomes more and more responsive to the aids (fig. 84).

Finally, through the concentration of forces achieved in collection, the rider will arrive, almost without realizing it, at Haute Ecole, the realm of equestrian tact and perfect lightness, the domain of perfection, of feeling, and of imponderables, the level at which the sport of riding becomes an art (fig. 85).